D0884100

CHIAROSCURO, AVENUE OF THE GIANTS

This is the land of

the last Redwoods

This is the last of an ancient race,
in a land of majestic forms . . .

SMITH RIVER, JEDEDIAH SMITH REDWOODS STATE PARK

. . . a land of serenity and grace,
evocative of a past long forgotten

REFLECTED ALDERS, RUSSIAN GULCH STATE PARK

PRAIRIE CREEK
REDWOOD STATE PARK

THE LAST REDWOODS

What would the world be, once bereft
Of wet and of wildness? Let them be left . . .

—GERARD MANLEY HOPKINS (from *Inversnaid*)

PHILIP HYDE
and FRANCOIS LEYDET

FOREWORD BY

Stewart L. Udall

Photographs and story of a vanishing scenic resource

SIERRA CLUB · SAN FRANCISCO

Publisher's Note: The book is set in Centaur and Arrighi by Mackenzie & Harris, Inc., San Francisco. The gravure is by Photogravure and Color Company and color by Barnes Press, Inc., New York City. It is bound in Columbia Mills' Sampson linen by Sendor Bindery, New York City. Design is by David Brower.

The Sierra Club, founded in 1892 by John Muir, has devoted itself to the study and protection of national scenic resources, particularly those of mountain regions. All Sierra Club publications are part of the nonprofit effort the club carries on as a public trust. The club is affiliated with the International Union for Conservation, the Natural Resources Council of America, and the Federation of Western Outdoor Clubs. There are chapters in California, the Pacific Northwest, the Great Basin, the Southwest, the Great Lakes region, and on the Atlantic seaboard. Participation is invited in the program to enjoy and preserve wilderness, wildlife, forests, and streams. *Address: Mills Tower, San Francisco; 25 West 45th Street, New York; 710 Dupont Circle Building, Washington, D. C.*

PUBLICATIONS COMMITTEE

AUGUST FRUGE, *Chairman,* GEORGE MARSHALL, *Vice Chairman*
DAVID BROWER, *Executive Director,* BRUCE M. KILGORE, *Secretary*
ANSEL ADAMS, FRANCIS P. FARQUHAR, MARTIN LITTON, ROBERT C. MILLER,
WALLACE STEGNER, EDGAR WAYBURN (*ex officio, president of the club*)

Copyright, 1963, by the Sierra Club   *Library of Congress Catalog Card No. 63-23018*
Manufactured in the United States of America

FOREWORD

In the beginning, the American continent nurtured arboreal stands as profuse and varied as any in the world: among over a hundred types of soft and hardwood trees were the oldest living things on the face of the earth (the bristlecone pines), the largest and tallest trees (the Sequoia and Redwoods of the Sierra and the California coast, the Douglas fir and the Sitka spruce) and such extraordinary specimens as the giant saguaro of the Arizona deserts and the bald cypress of the Everglades.

As a nation of woodsmen who made Paul Bunyan a national folklore hero we came late to the idea that our forests should be managed under a conservation plan that would ensure a long-term sustained yield of timber. We were equally late in developing the concept that some of our majestic woodlands should be preserved in their virgin state for all time as part of our National Park System.

Fortunately, though it came at a late hour, the ravaging of our woods had a reaction among Americans who loved the land. The concern and dedication of men like John Muir, and the gifts of persons like Congressman William Kent and his wife, who donated to the United States the groves that comprise the Muir Woods National Monument, saved little patches of fast-disappearing species.

In the Olympic National Park, Sequoia, Kings Canyon, Muir Woods, and elsewhere representative stands of the most majestic trees are now preserved, and under park management will provide inspiration and enjoyment for future generations of Americans.

The pressures of growth and the demands of commerce have caused the cutting of nearly all of the remaining virgin forests save those protected in state or federal parks—or bypassed because of the accident of being located in remote and rugged terrain.

Of the few remaining primeval forests in America the Redwoods of northern California have the strongest claim for permanent parkland status. It was no accident that the original forests of these magnificent trees were dubbed an "empire" by those who first marveled at their ranks. In the year of Columbus's landfall, 1492, the best estimates say there were 1,500,000 acres of Redwoods, an area comparable in size to Yosemite, Sequoia, and Kings Canyon National Parks combined. In 1918 when a group of leading scientists banded together to form the Save-the-Redwoods League, almost a third of the great trees had been cut. These conservation philanthropists won nation-wide support, and through their efforts to date 86,723 acres have been reserved as scenic sanctuaries where men may see the land in its pristine glory.

Sequoia sempervirens is one of the glories of our continent, and the groves that still stand are one of the overpowering pageants of nature. But we have learned, in managing the isolated enclaves of Redwoods now under state or federal protection, that no guardianship is sure unless a unit—a whole watershed—is placed under a single management plan that is ecologically sound.

In 1963 it will surprise no conservationist that John Muir's Sierra Club should raise a banner and lead the fight for a Redwoods National Park. Such a wilderness park will surely be established, if the eloquent words and pictures of this book arouse enough lovers of the land before it is too late.

STEWART L. UDALL

Washington, D. C., October, 1963

PUBLISHER'S NOTE

In 1912 E. C. Williams, last of the original quartet which started making redwood lumber commercially, reminisced in the *Mendocino Beacon* about his first prospecting for timber in the dark Sequoia wilderness of California's northern coast in 1850. It was spring as he took a rough redwood canoe up the Big River, bank full, "its slight ripples meeting the verdure of the shore, the tall redwoods with their great symmetrical trunks traveling toward the skies; with the bright colors of the rhododendrons profusely scattered over the hills forming the background, the clear blue sky above reflected in the placid river and over all the hush and solitude of the primeval forest—all combining to impress upon our minds the beauty and truth [in] Bryant's *Thanatopsis*, 'The groves were God's first temples.'"

Recalling the scene, he added "I cannot but regret the part it appeared necessary for me to enact in what now looks like a desecration."

There are no places left where one can duplicate Williams's experience of 1850. The banks of the rivers of the Redwood region which bore the stateliest stands of timber were the most accessible to early logging. But back along the feeder streams, shaded by willow and alder and too shallow to float a log, a few great stands of Sequoia sempervirens still remain. The best estimates we have are that the original redwood forests of California covered perhaps one and one half million acres in 1850. Today approximately four-fifths of the original forest is gone and the rate of its disappearance has accelerated. Less than five acres of each hundred of the original redwood forest is reserved in public ownership. This book speaks for those remaining trees, for their future and their meaning.

What will that future be? Williams made an estimate in 1912: "Doubtless a century or two hence someone rambling over the hills of (Mendocino County) will have his wonder excited by the immense stumps he sees—the relics of the stately trees which originally covered the hills and valleys with a forest unequaled in beauty."

What a legacy — to stir one's sense of wonder at a stump! If cutting continues at the present rate the observer will have little more than stumps to wonder at, not a century or two hence, but in no more than fifteen years. Today a traveler flying low over the Coast Ranges sees a vast tapestry of cut-over land: barren hillsides are interlaced with logging roads; skylines once silhouetting great forests are now punctuated only by an occasional snag; here and there a small island of rich dark green may float above the surrounding destruction, but the virgin redwood is almost gone.

In a sense, therefore, Philip Hyde and François Leydet have produced a requiem—a requiem for what we could have saved and didn't. This book is also a salute to the men of vision and generosity who did save some small part of a most superb natural heritage. Measured against what mankind might have done, it is a pitiful testimony. Measured as the accomplishment of these few men, it is enormous.

Most important, this book is a plea to take a good hard civilized look at what remains to be saved; not lamenting what we might have done, but considering what we can yet do. As of November 1963 a few areas north of Eureka still contain practically undisturbed redwood forests within watersheds intact enough to provide the redwoods reasonable protection—to preclude the kind of losses tragically initiated by logging upstream from the Rockefeller Forest on Bull Creek.

The price we must pay now to achieve a fraction of what we should have achieved many years ago will be high —some will think it excessively high —for we have waited a long time. But surely the richest nation in the world can afford, say, one ten-thousandth the price of a rocket to the treeless moon to capture and preserve an adequate fragment of a forest wonder that is the last of its kind on earth. Conservationists everywhere are grateful that Secretary Stewart Udall perceives the need and has stressed it in his foreword. Whatever we save will be not only for us, but also for the untold number to come who will deserve groves that are temples, and some chance to experience the wonder and beauty that Williams knew such a short time ago.

EDGAR WAYBURN
President, Sierra Club

San Francisco, November 15, 1963

ACKNOWLEDGMENTS

"Ecology" is a term with which the reader will meet more than once in this book. As defined in the dictionary, ecology is "the branch of biology which deals with the mutual relations between organisms and their environment." A Redwood grove, for instance, does not just happen as a result of a whim of nature. An ecological study of such a grove must take into consideration the complex interaction of climate, topography, soil, soil-fertilizing organisms, associated plants, and so forth. Disturb one element in the chain and you are likely to disturb them all—a truth which man, to his peril, has too long ignored in his treatment of the natural world.

It might not be too farfetched to speak of the "ecology" of this book. Like the Redwoods which it portrays, it is the end product of the interaction and coöperation of many forces—in this case people of varying backgrounds and expertise. It is the end result not only of the collaboration of the photographer and writer who are listed as co-authors, but also of contributions by many others without whose generous donation of time and energy and knowledge the book would be something other, and something less, than it is.

The authors' thanks go first to those who helped to assemble source materials for the book: to Josephine Moore, Plumas County Librarian, who obtained many reference books and other sources of information, some of them rare and difficult to locate; to Mrs. Frances Purser, Librarian of the Humboldt County Collection in the Library of Humboldt State College; to George Marshall of the Sierra Club, who in addition to his constant support of the project helped in assessing the material in the Huntington Library; and to Russell D. Butcher, who did much of the early research and thereby speeded the publication of the book by several months.

Invaluable because of their expert knowledge of Redwoods and of problems peculiar to the species and the region were Glen N. Jones, Superintendent of Prairie Creek Redwoods State Park, who was an on-the-spot fount of information and guidance; Carl Anderson of the Division of Beaches and Parks in Eureka, who besides sharing his knowledge made available the Division's maps; Ted Hatzimanolis of the United States Forest Service at Requa; Paul Zinke, Assistant Professor of Forestry at the University of California School of Forestry in Berkeley, who contributed much technical information; and Martin Litton, who provided not only information but advice, stimulation, and a feeling of urgency. Mr. Litton piloted the authors on two aerial trips over the Redwood region, joined them on a rowing trip down the Klamath River, and drove the writer of the text on a tour of the major Redwoods State Parks, all the while keeping up a steady monologue of information and observations from which more was learned than could be gathered in a month's research.

Again to Martin Litton go the authors' thanks for his close, sharp scrutiny of the manuscript, which is undoubtedly stronger for his remarks. Others who read and discussed it with the writer, and whose suggestions and corrections proved most valuable, were Dr. Edgar Wayburn, President of the Sierra Club; Russell Butcher; and David Brower, Executive Director of the Club.

One big debt of gratitude the authors owe is to the various photographers who made their pictures available to them: Ansel Adams, Moulin Studios, Florence Harrison, Madison Devlin, Harvey Richards, David Swanlund, Morley Baer, Marion Patterson, Wynn Bullock, Brett Weston, the California Division of Beaches and Parks; and Beaumont Newhall, Director of the George Eastman House in Rochester, who obtained for the authors the book *Redwood and Lumbering in California Forests* (San Francisco, 1884), from which photographs of early-day logging were reproduced. Thousands of photographs were considered before the final selection was made, and if all of the artists who made their pictures available are not represented in the book, it is not for lack of excellence of their work, but the need for particular photographs that would meet best the special purposes of the book.

Finally, the authors' thanks go to cartographer James Cutter, whose excellent maps graphically and artistically portray the original extent of the Redwoods' domain, and what is left of it today.

Indebted as they are to all who helped in one way or another toward the realization of this book, the authors, and they alone, are answerable for the opinions expressed in this work. More particularly, the writer-half of the collaboration, François Leydet, assumes full and sole responsibility for any errors of fact or interpretation that might be detected therein. They would be purely individual aberrations of which the "ecology" of the book must be absolved. P. H. and F. L.

CONTENTS

STUMP SPROUTS

Here is the stuff of immortality:
by the charred trunk new leaves
draw substance from ancient roots
and rise in a continuum.

1. LIFE OF AN IMMORTAL

Cradled in its moist bed of humus, the seed lay waiting. It was no bigger than the head of a match—a mere speck of vegetable matter. Yet locked within its tiny body were potent secrets: the secret of life, of a life force so determined that it might last to challenge the laws of mortality; and the secrets of growth—of growth so patient, so steady, so resourceful and relentless that it might some-day tower over all other living things.

These secrets, coded in its genes, the seed had inherited from its parent. That great tree, whose bole soared sky-ward some 100 feet away, was justifying its name of *Sequoia sempervirens*—ever-living Sequoia. For it had sprout-ed at the time when, in far-off Mesopotamia, Hammurabi was founding the Babylonian empire. By now Babylon had crumbled, and Hannibal of Carthage was leading his ele-phants across the Alps to throw the Roman Senate into panic. And still this hoary Coast Redwood stood, having filtered the sun and fogs of 1900 summers through its branches, having drunk the rains of 1900 winters through its roots.

In its genes, then, the seed had the potential to emulate its parent. But whether it would, in fact, do so depended on more than heredity. This, luck, fate, Providence would decide. Already, the seed had twice been blessed with luck. First it had been born viable, endowed with the spark of life. Of the thousands of seeds scattered the past winter by the parent tree, only a fourth or a third had been so endowed. Then, when the seed was released from its thimble-sized cone two hundred feet aloft among its par-ent's branches, the whims of air currents had chanced to deposit it at a spot on the forest floor where, when the time came, it could take root.

It did not have too long to wait. The warmth and dampness of the soil quickened its urge for life. Its outer covering split. Down went a tiny root; up into the light burst a frail opening shoot.

Fragile though it might be, the seedling from the first had all the beauty of its race. It grew straight and graceful. Its reddish-brown trunk was evenly wreathed with branches clad in a lovely foliage rather like a hemlock's. The twin-ranked leaves, dark green and glistening above, delicately silvered with lines of stomata below, grew in flat sprays that spread daintily outward like the hands of a girl drying her nails.

The young tree's guardsman-straight stance had a more than aesthetic purpose. Its unwavering aim was to grow up, up, up—up toward that narrow patch of sky that rent the canopy formed by the crowns of its elders, up into the life-giving light. It could afford to waste neither energy nor time in any deviation from its vertical surge. For it had competitors, and laggards would be crowded out.

This battle for supremacy and survival, obvious out in the open, was waged simultaneously on another front—underground. There, in the dark, its roots groped blindly outward, vying with others for water and nutrients of the soil. A Redwood sends out a wide-spreading net of shallow roots which serve both to nourish and support it, a system which in a mature tree may extend 40 to 50 feet away from its base, at four to six feet below the surface of the ground.

Over the decades, the sapling struggled on, fighting to maintain its claim for light and air and food against those of neighbors of its own and other generations. Did the life force flow just a whit more strongly within it than within its competitors? Was the particular patch of soil from which it drew its sustenance just a fraction more fertile? Was the half-light of the forest just a shade brighter upon it? Whatever the reason, it, and a few others, became established and thrived. The rest, weaker or less lucky, did not.

Year by year, our tree grew a little thicker and taller. Water and nutrient salts coursed up its trunk through the outer ring of yellow sapwood, were transformed in the leaves by photosynthesis into carbohydrates, which in turn passed down the sieve-like tubes of the inner bark to be used where needed for the tree's growth. Every year, the soft, protoplasm-filled inner cells of the cambium layer of living sapwood toughened and hardened, and a new band of red heartwood surrounded the old, forming what in cross section would appear as another ring.

The annual increase in height amounted only to inches —that in diameter to fractions of an inch. But by the time a young man of Nazareth began to preach his par-ables, our tree stood 100 feet tall and three feet through at the base. It had lost its early "Christmas tree" look; slightly fluted like an Ionic column, the trunk rose bare of branches for half its height. The tree by now had passed the 200-year mark. But at an age which in many species would be venerable it was a mere adolescent.

Two more centuries passed. Safely over the continuing crisis of infancy and childhood, the tree had in those years more than doubled its height and girth. The most dramatic happening had been an unusually violent lightning storm, in which a bolt had exploded in the crown of the parent tree, setting it ablaze. The fire had flickered and smouldered for days, and by the time it had burned itself out the old giant was fatally weakened. Occasional windstorms hit with hurricane force, and a few more-exposed veterans came crashing down. In one of these storms the parent tree was toppled.

Presently our young tree met with a new experience. While the first serious irruptions of Germanic tribes into the Roman Empire were beginning, soon to wax into a flood, forces of a different kind were in motion out over the Pacific. A great circling mass of air, heavily laden with rain clouds, began to spiral eastward, towards the coast of what men (who had yet to dream of America, let alone a Sequoia) would one day call Northern California. When the clouds hit the coastal ranges they opened up. For days, for a week, for a month the deluge raged unabated.

At the foot of a steep forested slope, our tree stood on the edge of a "flat," a high river bench built up by past floods. Now, as the storm continued, the river once again overtopped its banks. Throughout its watershed, swollen creeks collected the runoff from saturated hillsides and added their loads to its stream. Up the trunks of the Redwoods in the flat the river's waters rose, thick and soupy with silt.

Finally the storm played itself out, the sun broke through, and the waters receded. But the forest floor was no longer recognizable. In place of the green carpet of fern and oxalis and moss there stretched a flat, bare, gray expanse of silt. What was more, the ground level had risen nearly three feet. Trunks of the bigger trees seemed somewhat shrunken, as now their butt swells were buried in the mud.

For our tree, as for its fellows, this new situation was serious: A Redwood's roots have to lie near the surface. But part of the information once locked in the tiny seed was the knowledge of how to cope with just such a challenge as this. The tree began to develop a new and higher root system, and as this took over the job of feeding and supporting it, the older roots were allowed to die.

Another, more serious, crisis overtook the tree a century later. The previous summer had been unusually hot and fog-free; and winter's rains, which in normal years swept in from the ocean in storm after drenching storm, had been intermittent and perfunctory. The drought had persisted through the spring and into this summer. In the

evenings, no billows of fog came rolling in over the hills across the river, to cool the air and replace the forest's moisture that had evaporated during the day: The fog bank stayed far out to sea, a gray shape crouched on the horizon like a whipped animal. The sun would rise in a clear sky, bake the land all day, and long after it had sunk behind the hills high cirrus clouds shone rose and gold, reflecting its dying rays.

Up in the hills the creeks ran dry, and an unwonted number of deer, bear and other back-country dwellers crossed the flat to the shrunken river for a drink. The undergrowth was sere and brown, fern fronds snapped off as an animal brushed by them, and the normally sponge-like litter of decaying leaves and needles was light and dry as desert dust.

The fire, when it came, was brutal. Anything young, tender or low-growing was turned to ashes and charcoal. The flames burned deep into the desiccated humus, and in the super-heated air, tongues of fire leaped high up the trunks of the big Redwoods. These needed every inch of their thick, asbestos-like bark to protect them from hurt, nor was it always quite enough. The fire was particularly hot on the slope-facing side of our tree, where debris that had rolled or washed down from the hill lay deep. The bark turned black, then red, then incandescent, and the flames licked at the living sapwood.

Our tree was left with a great, charcoal-covered wound, five feet wide at its base, 15 feet high, shaped like a gothic arch. At ground level a quarter of the sapwood and inner bark essential for life and growth had been destroyed. But though severe, the wound was not fatal, and the tree immediately set about healing the scar.

Inch by inch, year by year, new bark and tissue grew out over the edges of the blackened area. Occasionally a smaller fire, invading the forest, attacked the injured part and interrupted or set back the healing process. But with all the vigor and tenacity that had allowed it first to establish itself against competition, later to adapt to the changes brought about by the flood, the tree persisted in repairing the damage. Within a century, its girdle of bark was restored, and it could return to the century-to-century business of living and growing and producing seed.

By the year 800 A.D., when Charlemagne was crowned Emperor of the Holy Roman Empire, our tree had lived its first millenium. By the time architects and stone masons and sculptors and glaziers in Western Europe were erecting those sublime cathedrals to whose lofty pillared naves Redwood groves have been likened, our tree was 1500 years old.

Five times floods had raised the level of the ground.

Five times the tree had grown a new system of roots. Twice since that first fierce blaze it had been scarred by fire. Each time it had drawn on its endless regenerative power and had closed its wounds. Its huge ribbed trunk, now 15 feet through at the base, rose more than 200 feet straight up to the first downward-sweeping branches. For the next 100 feet it was clad in foliage. This was no thick, bushy spread of needles as might have seemed fitting to a tree of its size, but still the delicate, feminine sprays that adorned it as a sapling—except at the very top, 320 feet up, where its crown broke through the canopy of the forest and where short, awl-shaped needles bore a striking resemblance to those of its cousin, the Big Tree of the Sierra.

Old the tree was—old by human standards, old by the standards of almost all life but its own. And yet it was in the full prime of maturity. On and on it thrived, adding imperceptibly every year to its height and its girth, while men fought crusades and wars, Columbus discovered America, the Pilgrims landed at Plymouth Rock, the Thirteen Colonies broke away from British rule. On and on it lived, while great forests across the continent were being laid low by axe and plough.

It was in 1849, the year of the Argonauts, the year of the great stampede to the Sierra gold fields, that the tree was presented with its most deadly challenge. A fire, greater than any that it had suffered and survived, burned through the foot-thick bark, through the sapwood and even into the heartwood for a third of its circumference, leaving an enormous 17-foot-wide scar. Worse yet, the fire killed all the roots on that side of the tree.

As time went on, our tree began to list towards the north, the side on which the roots had been killed. The list gradually became more pronounced, until the top was 40 feet north of the base. It seemed that, after more than 2000 years of life, the tree must shortly fall.

In this extremity, that powerful will to live, the extraordinary secrets of survival that had all been sealed in the little seed came into play in the most amazing way yet. As before, the tree began to heal the scar from each side. But from the side nearest the falling axis, it also started to build out a strong supporting buttress to take over from the now useless roots.

As if it knew that its life was in peril, the tree poured its energy into extending that buttress, pushing it forward half an inch a year—which was far faster than it was increasing its girth in any other direction. A race was on between the tree and the weather: Could the buttress be built out far enough to give it firm support before a major storm could upset it?

Ten, twenty, fifty, a hundred years rolled by, and still our tree stood firm. The buttress now projected four feet; as every winter struck, it had advanced a little farther towards the north, giving the leaning tree that much more support. Then came the winter of 1955.

Just before the end of the year, a storm of epic proportions swirled in from the ocean—a storm that was to cause landslides, raging floods and major devastation throughout northern California. For days the rain came down in torrents; it poured off the saturated hillside behind the tree into the flat. The soil around the tree became soft, sodden, boggy. With no firm ground under it, the buttress no longer could hold the tree's 1000 tons.

The end came in the early hours of the morning of December 26th. Slowly at first, the lofty trunk leaned farther out of plumb. There was a tearing sound, as roots parted under the strain, and a sucking noise, as the butt pulled free of the earth. Gathering momentum, amid a great sigh as the air parted before it, the tree crashed down. Nearly 2200 years from the day when its first green shoot had poked up into the sunlight, it lay sprawled for its full 350 feet across the earth from which it had sprung.

And so the old monarch died. And yet it did not. For the roots that had severed when it had started its fall lay there beneath the ground, and within them still coursed the same flow of life. Early in the spring, up from these same roots, up into the life-giving light rose a dozen fresh shoots. These were not a new generation from seed: They were a continuation of the same tree life. They were the old tree itself, which had been metamorphosed into these new shapes. Through them it could live on and grow —Sequoia sempervirens, the ever-living.

2. REDWOODS THROUGH THE AGES

Standing at the foot of a giant Redwood, craning your neck to look up the soaring trunk, you sense your puniness. This tree, you are told, is probably well over a thousand years old. You are impressed, but you do not fully grasp the meaning of this figure until you reduce it to human terms, until you calculate that this tree was alive when William conquered England; that while forty, perhaps fifty generations of humans lived and loved and fought and died, this tree always stood in this very place, aloof and mindless of human antics.

No such convenient scale exists to help us comprehend the age of the Redwoods as a race. Long before the first pre-humans lived, the Redwoods were there. Before the first small mammal had evolved, the Redwoods were there. Before the original primitive ancestors of most of today's plants had developed, the Redwoods were there.

The first positively identified Redwood fossils, represented by characteristic cones, date back to the Upper Jurassic period—some 130 million years ago. Could a man be transported back to those times, there would be little about him that he would recognize. The continents had not yet taken their present forms. The stresses had yet to build up in the earth's crust that would thrust up our great mountain chains, the Alps, the Himalayas, the Rockies, the Andes.

A strange fauna then inhabited the earth. Swarms of sharks and ganoid fishes, huge marine reptiles—serpent-like plesiosaurs, dolphin-like ichthyosaurs—prowled the seas. Flying reptiles, which in the next period, the Cretaceous, would reach wingspreads of 15 to 20 feet, circled overhead. Dinosaurs of gigantic size and weird shapes were the lords of the land.

The flora was equally strange—great ferns, an enormous variety of cycads, and the many ancestors of that living fossil of today, the ginkgo or maidenhair tree. There were as yet no angiosperms, the flowering plants that dominate the vegetable kingdom today. But among all these bizarre and now long-vanished forms of life, the Redwoods flourished.

Through 60 million years of the Cretaceous period, down into the Tertiary, they thrived and extended their sway, while the world's flora and fauna were being radically remade. Species after species of the dull-witted, clumsy reptiles declined and became extinct. The age of mammals had begun. The little eohippus—the four-toed ancestor of the horse—primitive rhinoceroses, tapirs and camels, the forebears of the cat and dog tribes, inherited the earth. The plants, too, were changing. Broad-leafed conifers, juniper-like evergreen, then, later, hardwood trees such as the oaks and maples, hickory and ash we know today, displaced the earlier dominants.

By the Miocene, which began 25 million years ago, the "Redwood Empire" stretched across the northern hemisphere—from western Canada to the Atlantic, from France to Japan. In the United States, fossil remains of Redwoods have been found in Texas, Pennsylvania, Colorado, Wyoming, Oregon, Washington, and California. In Yellowstone National Park, whole forests have been changed to stone by the mineral waters, or buried in showers of ashes from active volcanoes in the vicinity; sections of the trunks are 6 to 10 feet in diameter, and the butts still stand just as they grew, often 30 feet or more in height. In the Petrified Forest of Sonoma County are giant logs that were buried and turned to stone.

The Arctic was then no land of snow and ice, but rather a humid and temperate region, and Redwood fossils have been found in Spitzbergen, in Greenland, on many of the Arctic islands north of the continent of North America, in Alaska and on St. Lawrence Island. Of the latter discovery Dr. Ralph Chaney, Professor of Paleontology at the University of California, wrote in his pamphlet *Redwoods of the Coast:*

"One of the most significant places where fossil Redwoods have been found in the Far North is on St. Lawrence Island, in the Bering Sea, midway between Alaska and Siberia. It is too cold and windy for trees of any sort to grow there today, but in long ages past there flourished upon it a forest as beautiful as that of the Redwood Belt (in California). St. Lawrence Island is a portion of the land connection between Asia and North America, over which the Redwood and many other plants have migrated from one continent to the other, along with the dinosaur, rhinoceros and other animals of the prehistoric past . . ." (including, he might add, eventually man himself.)

The Redwoods in those times were as varied as they were far-flung. Paleobotanists have identified at least a dozen species. One, *Sequoia Reichenbachi,* found in Cretaceous clays, had cones almost like those of the Big Trees

FOREST EDGE, BULL CREEK FLAT

EEL RIVER NEAR WEOTT

MILL CREEK, JEDEDIAH SMITH REDWOODS STATE PARK

FIVE-FINGER FERNS

FOREST AISLES, BULL CREEK FLAT

RUSSIAN RIVER NEAR RIO NIDO

of the Sierra. The most common, *Sequoia Langsdorfii,* was almost indistinguishable from the modern *Sequoia sempervirens.* Still another, otherwise similar to the Coast Redwood, had the peculiarity that its twigs and cones had an opposite arrangement, whereas *Sequoia sempervirens* shows a spiral attachment of the twigs, needles and cone-scales; also its cones grew at the end of naked stalks instead of on needle-bearing twigs. To this fossil Redwood was given the generic name *Metasequoia,* the Dawn Redwood, to distinguish it from the true Sequoias.

With the close of the Miocene, the Redwoods began to retreat. Over millions of years the climate grew colder and drier. The Arctic became chill, then frozen, and where dense forests had stood, only lichens, dwarf willows, and sphagnum moss clothed the ground above the permafrost. Great icecaps formed, and in time the glaciers advanced to the south, inexorably bulldozing everything in their way. In Europe, where they had formed forests in England, France, Germany, Bohemia, Austria, Switzerland, the Redwoods withdrew before the glaciers until they were backed up against the Mediterranean—a Dunkirk in slow motion. Only there was no evacuation for them, no way by which they could escape across to Africa. And so they perished.

In Asia, land of the Dawn Redwood, the story was the same—or so it was thought until 1944. In that year, a forester chanced across an immense tree in a remote village of Szechuan province in central China. He had never seen one like it, so he brought out with him samples of twigs and cones. To their amazement, experts found them to be identical with *Metasequoia* fossil specimens gathered in Manchuria and Japan. Here, indeed, was a spectacular discovery: a fossil come to life, a tree thought dead for 25 million years but still growing, as it turned out, by the hundreds in an isolated region of Szechuan and neighboring Hupeh provinces. In this one small area, where conditions of temperature and humidity were just right, this tree which once reigned from the Black Sea to Greenland had made its last stand.

In America, too, the Redwood Empire shrank. The southward march of the glaciers, great volcanic eruptions, and the upthrust of mountain ranges singly and collectively undid the work of 100 million years. In eastern Oregon, for instance, there had stood a mixed forest of Dawn Redwoods and of the immediate ancestors of our modern Coast Redwoods. Then the Cascades reared up their fiery summits in the path of the ocean winds. Today, eastern Oregon is an arid land, with rainfall sufficient only for the growth of scattered juniper trees and sagebrush.

As the Redwoods' domain shrank, so did the number of their species. In time just two were left, and as it happened, California was where they both made their last bid for survival. The Big Tree, *Sequoia gigantea,* standing in isolated groves in the southern Sierra Nevada, and the Redwood, *Sequoia sempervirens,* occupying a narrow strip along the northern California coast, are the last representatives of an heroic race, the last of the true Sequoias, a living link to the age of dinosaurs.

3. TITANS OF THE COAST

By their age, by their size, by their majestic beauty, the Sequoias of California's coast and Sierra represent Nature's supreme achievement in the evolution of trees. No other race of trees comes close to matching them. Nowhere else on earth are there groves or forests that compare with California's stands of Sequoias.

Because of the Sequoias' preëminence, because so many superlatives apply fittingly to both species, and because the two types live naturally in California and nowhere else (except a few Coast Redwoods in extreme southwestern Oregon)—it is normal that some confusion between the two should have resulted in peoples' minds. Many probably assume that the coast and Sierra giants are the same tree, growing in two different localities. They are not. There is sufficient difference between them, in fact, for some botanists to have suggested that the Sierra Big Tree be given a different generic name, *Sequoiadendron giganteum* instead of *Sequoia gigantea*, reserving the name *Sequoia (sempervirens)* for its cousin of the coast.

Each of the two species has had its champions. John Muir, for one, was prejudiced in favor of the Sierra's Big Trees. Bret Harte went so far in his partisanship as to refer to the Coast Redwoods as the "poor relations" of the mountain species. In sheer craggy grandeur, in individual impressiveness, the Big Trees are without peer.

They are the biggest of all living things, and nearly the oldest—only the fantastic, gnarled bristlecone pine, whose wind-tortured shapes grow high in the White Mountains of California and other Great Basin ranges, is known to exceed the Big Tree's maximum lifespan of 4,000 years. In contrast, the greatest recorded age, by actual ring count, of a Coast Redwood is 2200 years. Though averaging 50 feet less in height than its coastal relatives—the tallest known giant Sequoia, the California tree, measures 310 feet—it far surpasses them in girth and weight. Whereas mature Coast Redwoods average 12 to 16 feet in diameter, and none quite reaches 23 feet, hundreds of Big Trees are more than 25 feet through at the base, many reach 30 to 32 feet, and the General Grant, the world's thickest tree, has a base diameter of 40.3 feet and circumference of 107.6. The General Sherman tree, presumed to be the world's "largest living thing," weighs an estimated 6167 tons; one of its limbs is larger than most of the trees in the Rocky Mountains.

On the other hand, "The Redwood, the ever-living Sequoia, sempervirens, is the tallest tree in the world," writes Donald Culross Peattie in *A Natural History of Western Trees*. "Not just occasionally taller, in individual specimens growing under unprecedently favorable conditions, but taller as a whole, as a race, a titan race." Yet as you walk among the Redwoods, it is not so much the size of an individual tree that awes you into silence. It is rather the impact of the forest as a whole, of the overwhelming ambiance of gigantism. For immensity is all about. There stands in Dyerville Flat a tree known as the Founders' Tree, dedicated to John C. Merriam, Henry Fairfield Osborn, and Madison Grant, founders of the Save-the-Redwoods League. This was long thought to be the tallest tree in the world until it was remeasured, and the title passed to a 359-foot giant in the Rockefeller Forest on Bull Creek Flat. But were it not for the signs pointing it out and the low fence about its base one would not single out the Founders' Tree for particular attention. It is only one titan in a legion of titans.

The tallest of trees is related closely to the greatest of oceans. From extreme southwestern Oregon to the Santa Lucia mountains below Carmel, the Redwood forest extends for 450 miles in a narrow belt, averaging 20 miles in width. Sometimes growing right to the Pacific shore, sometimes swinging inland for 30 or 40 miles as it follows the line of the Coast Ranges, the Redwood never strays from the realm of the ocean winds.

At the south end of their range, in the Santa Lucias, the trees are confined to deep narrow canyons where streams and springs and shade compensate for the dry climate. Here the stand is thin, the trees scattered or isolated, and individual trees assume uncharacteristic shapes, with very long branches or irregular crowns or even flat tops.

Farther up the coast, in the Santa Cruz mountains, and, north of the Golden Gate Bridge, in the canyons of Marin and Sonoma and Mendocino counties, the Redwoods grow more thickly, and there are many large, well-shaped trees. But it is mainly farther north, in Humboldt and Del Norte counties, that the trees today reach their full stature, the forest its full glory. Here the winter rains are heaviest, ranging from 50 to 100 inches a year. And here the thickest fogs roll in on summer evenings to saturate the atmosphere and check evaporation from the leaves.

The relationship of climate and Redwoods is a reciprocal one. So tall are the trees, so dense is the forest, that the Redwoods themselves act as a climatic force. "No one can as yet tell the extent of this influence, but my personal feeling is that it is considerable," writes British forester and silviculturist Richard St. Barbe Baker, founder of The Men of the Trees. ". . . The Redwoods condense and filter out drops of water from the coast mists, which are often heaviest in the driest summers. This so-called horizontal precipitation may be of considerable benefit to the growth of plant life as well as the trees themselves, and could turn what might be barren land without them, into a state of fertility."

Were the forest not there to intercept and trap their moisture, the fogs would probably benefit neither plant, beast, nor man. There would be no rich undercover, no deep sponge-like layer of decomposing leaves and needles to act as a reservoir, to keep the springs and creeks flowing in summer and to dam and regulate the overflow of water during winter storms. Without the anchoring power of the Redwoods' great spreading roots and of the myriad tiny roots of plants that grow in their shade, the friable earth of the steep hillsides would wash into the gullies. Depending on the season, streams would be dry arroyos or raging, muddy torrents, and the salmon, steelhead, and trout would go elsewhere to spawn.

Much Redwood country is rugged country. The coast giants do not adapt to high altitudes or snow; unlike the Big Trees of the Sierra, which grow at altitudes of 5000 to 8000 feet undisturbed by zero temperatures or deep snow drifts, the Redwood never climbs above 3000 feet. But if it boasts of no soaring peaks, this is still a sharply etched land, a land of high ridges and deep valleys. Its geological history makes its soils highly unstable, ever ready to seek a lower level, to be washed out to sea. It is a land of lovely, clear creeks, like Mill Creek, Blue Creek, Prairie Creek and Redwood Creek, and, once upon a time, Bull Creek; bigger rivers such as the Russian River, the two Eels, and the Smith, coursing swift and strong in winter, or flowing serene between sand-and-gravel banks in summer's low-water months; and greatest of the lot, the deep, powerful Klamath.

It is finally an oceanic land both geographically and climatically. The tidal flux is never far away, and the influence of the sea is all-pervasive. The coast itself varies greatly in character. Along the Mendocino county shores, the combers boil and froth around the rocks and stacks offshore, or dash themselves against the rugged cliffline, deeply indented by narrow coves. Farther north the swells wash onto broad, straight beaches, piled high with driftwood. Behind the strands and dunes stretch peaceful lagoons, alive with the cries of waterfowl, or high bluffs with a dark crown of trees.

Throughout this region the Redwood is king (or was before man altered much of the face of the land). But the aspect of the forest changes constantly—from slopes to flats, from streamside to seacoast. It changes also from south to north—as the climate becomes wetter, the undergrowth becomes lusher, more tangled and exuberant.

On the seaward edge of its belt, the Redwood shares its domain with several magnificent species of conifers, such as the coast hemlock, the Sitka or tidelands spruce, the lowland fir and Lawson's cypress. On the slopes, at the heads of canyons or on the divides, the Redwood admits the company of other trees—the Douglas fir, itself a noble tree which farther north, in Washington, attains a height of 325 feet; the aggressive tan oak; the madrone, with shiny green leaves and bright red satiny limbs. Shrubs grow thick in places—the California rosebay with its stunning rose-purple blooms; the fragrant western azalea; berry bushes like the California huckleberry, the thimbleberry with large velvety yellow-green leaves and downy bright red berries, the salmon berry with its luscious yellow fruit. Here and there a poison oak will climb a Redwood trunk to heights of 50 to 150 feet, and to the human trespasser its autumnal riot of flaming leaves is aesthetic atonement for its toxicity.

The stream banks too have their own characteristic species. Here the bigleaf maple glows golden in the fall; the sunlight shimmers through thickets of red alders; mosses robe the tree trunks and beard their boughs; the five-finger fern hangs lovely fronds from the banks.

It is along the streams that wildlife, or the signs of its presence, can most often be seen. A black bear patrolling a sandy bank at dusk. A river beaver swimming downstream with a branch in its mouth, trailing a V-shaped wake. A great blue heron poised motionless at the water's edge, its sharp beak set to strike, or taking flight with a squawk, head tucked back and long legs trailing, and flapping its way to a roost high in a Redwood's limbs. A startled mother merganser taking off low across the water, followed by her brood of ducklings frantically beating their stubby wings, not quite able yet to become airborne. A sharp-taloned osprey circling overhead on the alert for an unwary fish.

In the morning, the sand and mudbanks are like a hotel register, inscribed with the signatures of the visitors of the night: the delicate pointed hoofprints of deer, the great flat-footed, sharp-clawed tracks of bear, the small handlike prints of raccoon, occasionally the doglike tracks of a coyote or the rounded marks of a bobcat's soft pads.

Along the larger streams and rivers the Redwoods form a solid curtain, shielding from prying eyes the mysteries of the forest. Here the great trees are limbed from crown to ground, and the protective screen of their foliage deflects the hurrying wind. Turn your back to the rippled stream, to the dancing light playing on the waters, part the leafy curtain, and you enter another world where time and space assume new dimensions.

It is on these river-side "flats," often found at the confluence of two streams and built up gradually by the floods of the ages, that the Redwood forest achieves a quintessence of majesty, an aura of holiness. There is something Olympian about the trees' massed ranks—if ever there were gods of trees, here they stand.

Away in all directions extend the vaulted naves. The ruddy pillars soar straight up, mighty beyond description, a mightiness that defies capture on printed page or photographic plate. Their buttressed bases seem to grip the earth with great leonine claws. Here and there a lumpy swelling mars the symmetry of a trunk. These huge burls, of unknown cause, sometimes resemble weird animals' heads, and you feel transported back to the dawn of time, watching a tyrannosaurus scratch its armored head against the bark.

The thick layer of needles and moss cushions your footsteps. The shamrock leaves and pretty pink-lavender blossoms of the redwood sorrel, oxalis, carpet the forest floor as far as the eye can see. The many ferns, which grow luxuriantly from every hummock and every fallen trunk often attain great stature. The flowering plants for the most part hug the soil; their blossoms are usually small, inconspicuous, even minute. But they can bloom in such profusion that they change the whole atmosphere of the forest. Sometimes acres and acres are covered with the myriad tiny, pure white flowers of the sugar scoop, and then the aisles glow with a soft, strange light, as if the Milky Way had come to rest on the forest floor. Many of these little plants bear poetic names which strung together sound like a nosegay poor, mad Ophelia might have picked: deer-foot, fringe-cup, inside-out flower, bleeding heart, milk-maid, fairy lantern, slim Solomon, fat Solomon, phantom orchis.

The light in the depths of the forest is dim and muted as it filters down from the canopy two or three hundred feet above. High overhead the lace-work of needles constantly changes patterns as it is ruffled by the wind—now closing up, then parting to reveal a patch of blue; here fragmenting the sun's rays into a thousand pearls of light, there letting through a slanting shaft like that from a church's stained glass window. Where touched by the sun, the Redwood's dark needles glow with a golden sheen. Even in the thickest fog, the aura of the forest is mysterious rather than forbidding; then the great trunks loom out of the mists with an unreal air, ghosts from a forgotten past.

The silence, too, is the silence of peace and of strength, of beings living at ease with their past and secure in their future. It is a silence that communicates itself to the human intruder, that makes him hush his voice and stills all shrillness in him. Only the blue-crested Steller's jay, as brash of manner as he is gaudy of plumage, proclaims his irreverence in a raucous voice. "The tiny, somber-clad winter wren slips through the fern levels, his high, cascading song pouring musically from luxuriant depths," writes John Lindsey Blackford. "At intervals the mystery-strain of the varied thrush rings amid these fathomless solitudes. While haunting the underwood, the ashen-hued hermit thrush is more than ever only an ecstatic voice."

From somewhere high above comes the creak and rasp of branch rubbing against branch. "And now and then," recounts Peattie, "the treetops utter a slow, distant sea-hush, a sigh that passes, and then comes again, as if it were the breathing of a life beside which our lives are as a single day."

Time, time as we dissect it in days and hours and minutes, loses all meaning in a setting such as this. Here is a forest that was young when life itself was young. Here are trees that have already stood for a millenium or two—and still their lives will outlast yours a thousand years.

Of a forest such as this Duncan McDuffie wrote: "To enter the grove of Redwoods on Bull Creek Flat is to step within the portals of a cathedral dim, lofty, pillared, peaceful.

"But this temple which the Great Architect has been building for a score of centuries is incomparably nobler, more beautiful and more serene than any erected by the hands of man. Its nave is loftier than that of Amiens and longer than that of St. Peter's. Its wine-red shafts, rising clean and straight over two hundred feet, are more numerous than the pillars of Cordova; its floor is carpeted with a green and brown mosaic more intricate than that of St. Mark's; its aisles are lit with a translucence more beautiful than that which filters through the stained glass of Chartres; its spires pierce higher than those of Cologne; its years are greater than those of the first lowly building devoted to Christian service.

"To destroy this noblest of places of worship would be more irreparable than was the destruction of the cathedral of Rheims."

Just such destruction is what we must now explore.

REALM OF THE OCEAN WINDS

From the sea winds the trees came,
and to it like gulls they belong,
in a world where what is cool and wet prevails,
and its special wildness

GOLD BLUFFS BEACH

COAST NEAR ELK, MENDOCINO COUNTY

PRIVATE TIMBERLAND ADJACENT TO JEDEDIAH SMITH REDWOODS STATE PARK

PALO COLORADO

MAPLES, PRAIRIE CREEK REDWOODS STATE PARK

POOL ON EAST RIDGE ROAD, PRAIRIE CREEK REDWOODS STATE PARK

SMITH RIVER NEAR JEDEDIAH SMITH REDWOODS STATE PARK

STOUT GROVE, JEDEDIAH SMITH REDWOODS STATE PARK

NELSON GROVE, HUMBOLDT REDWOODS STATE PARK

4. THE HAND OF MAN

One of the Redwood's mysteries is that it seems to have no natural lifespan. There is no biological reason known why one should ever die. The tannin which impregnates its bark and heartwood and gives them their rich red color makes the tree impervious to attacks of insects or fungi. The Redwood normally is immune to ordinary tree diseases—accidental death is its usual fate. Despite the Redwood's marvelous resistance to fire, fire can kill it, or so weaken it that a storm will overthrow it. Great winds will topple the more exposed trees. Ecological changes, too, can shorten a Redwood's life—such as the compaction of the soil over its roots, or the interruption by one cause or another of the seepage of groundwater.

Over the ages, forces of climate and geology have reduced the Redwoods to a small fraction of their former domain. It is possible that the same forces, of themselves, could in the end cause the total extinction of this ancient race—although they could just as well work to the Redwoods' advantage and allow the trees to re-colonize lands once occupied by them.

Today, however, the Redwoods face a more immediate threat than fire or tempest or frost or volcanic ash. Their greatest enemy, the most ruthless and methodical destroyer of the forests, is that animal which by its extraordinary abilities has become a geological force in its own right—modern Man.

The first men to live among the Redwoods had little effect on the forest. The Indians certainly started an occasional forest fire. Amazingly, they even did some logging, felling the giant trees without the use of a single metal tool. Using heated stones, they would burn a hole on one side of the tree, scraping off the charcoal with elkhorn tools until enough of the tree was cut away. Then a hole was made on the other side of the trunk, a little higher up. The Indians were skillful enough to be able to fell the tree in a given direction, and while one group made the cuts, another placed logs on the ground for a bed to receive the trunk as it fell. The same process of burn-and-scrape was used to buck the trunk into sections, after which boards were made by driving wedges of wood and elkhorn into the ends, splitting the logs into planks. These then were smoothed with stone adzes.

All this was naturally a slow, laborious process, and a Redwood plank would become a treasured possession—even being handed down as an heirloom from one generation to the next. With such methods the Indians could do little to the forest as a whole. Lightning started more fires than they, and wind and rain claimed many times more trees.

Nor did the early white men have much impact on the Redwoods. The first to see the trees were probably the Portolá expedition, the first Spaniards to explore the California coast by land. On October 10, 1769, Fray Juan Crespi, chronicler of the expedition, recorded in his diary that on the Pajaro river near present-day Watsonville the party travelled "over plains and low hills, well forested with very high trees of a red color, not known to us. . . . In this region there is a great abundance of these trees and because none of the expedition recognizes them, they are named Redwood (*palo colorado*) from their color. We stopped near a lagoon which has pasture about and a heavy growth."

On March 26, 1776, Fray Pedro Font, the diarist of de Anza's expedition to San Francisco Bay, reported that they had seen "a few trees which they call Redwood, a tree that is certainly beautiful; and I believe (he added prophetically) that it is very useful for its timber for it is very straight and tall. . . " Three days later, on the return journey, de Anza's men spied in the distance "a very high Redwood . . . rising like a great tower." Reaching it the following day Font measured it: "I found it to be . . . fifty *varas* high (137 feet 6 inches), a little more or less. The trunk at the foot was five and a half varas (14 feet 9 inches) in circumference and the soldiers said they had seen even larger ones in the mountains." Font's tall tree, his "*palo alto*," still stands today, and from it the town of Palo Alto took its name.

Despite Brother Font's accurate estimate of its value as lumber, the Spaniards made light use of the Redwood, preferring to build in adobe. They did employ a few heavy beams in their churches and mission buildings, and history records that at his request Padre Junípero Serra, founder of California's chain of missions, was buried in 1784 in a Redwood coffin at Mission San Carlos Borromeo in Carmel. Long lost in the church's ruins, the coffin was rediscovered 98 years after the burial, and found to be still in perfect condition.

The Russians, in pursuit of the sea otter, established in 1812 a colony at Fort Ross on the Mendocino coast, and remained there until 1841 when the near-extinction of the otters and the failure of attempts at trade and agriculture decided the Russian-American Company of Alaska to sell its interest in the "Colony Ross" to Captain John Sutter of Sacramento. The Russians' buildings and stockade were made of Redwood, and their chapel, built of hand-hewn Redwood timbers, still stands to this day.

But it was not until the Gold Rush that the Redwoods began to feel the hand of man. Even then, with timber for building purposes exceedingly scarce, Redwood at first was regarded with contempt because of its softness, lightness and relative lack of strength. Houses were brought "around the Horn" and set up in San Francisco and Oakland—one was even taken to Trinidad, in the very heart of the northern Redwoods. Nor did the first overland explorers of the "Redwood Belt" always show much appreciation of the beauty of their surroundings. Rogers and Wood, for instance, in their journal *The Quest for Qual-A-Wa-Loo,* described their experience in traversing the area just east of Trinidad:

"The timber in this part of this country is principally hemlock (spruce), pine (Douglas fir) and white cedar (the Redwood), the most of the cedar trees from 5 to 15 feet in diameter, and tall in proportion to the thickness, the underbrush, hazle, oak, briars, currants, gooseberry, and Scotch cap bushes, together with alder, and sundry other shrubs too tedious to mention; the soil of the country rich and black, but very mountainous, which renders travelling almost impassible (sic) . . .

"Through this forest we could not travel to exceed two miles a day. The reason of this was the immense quantity of fallen timber that lay upon the ground in every conceivable shape and direction and in many instances one piled upon another so that the only alternative left was literally to cut our way through . . . For three long weary days did we toil in these Redwoods. Exhaustion and almost starvation had reduced the animals to the last extremity.

"At length we issued from this dismal forest prison in which we had so long been shut up, into the open country, and at the same instant in full view of that vast world of water—the Pacific Ocean."

Despite their original prejudice against it, the Forty-Niners made use of Redwood because of its abundance and cheapness. And they soon found that it had more to commend it than price alone. "As timber the Redwood is too good to live," was John Muir's bitter comment. The wood has many of the same properties as the tree, and as a result the very qualities which protected the tree in the forest condemned it to destruction by man. Durable in contact with earth or water, rot- and termite-proof, non-warping, retentive of paint and easy to work, Redwood was cut for everything from houses to wharf piles, from barns to sluice boxes, fences to water tanks, pipelines to shakes and shingles. And to top it all, the wood was almost as handsome as the tree. "As a wood for fine panelling it is a beauty," writes Peattie. "The heartwood needs no coloring but its own natural soft rich hue. More, it has an inexplicable golden gloss of its own, an halation as delicate as the shimmer on a tress of blond hair."

As early as 1850 sawmills were installed on the hills, south of San Francisco, which soon became a city of Redwood houses. The stands of Redwood on the Peninsula were heavily cut; in the East Bay hills, where their outline against the sky had been a landmark for ship captains entering the Golden Gate, the magnificent trees were logged off within a decade. In 1855 the first shipment by sea went from Humboldt county to San Francisco.

The Redwoods were not cut only for their lumber. To many a hardy homesteader the great trees were but a nuisance, overgrown weeds to be cut or burned or rooted up. The laws of the time reflected the prevailing philosophy that the important thing was to get the land "settled up." And so, under the Pre-emption Law of 1841 and the Homestead Act of 1862 the bona fide settler could purchase 160 acres of Redwood timberland at $1.25 an acre—no more than he would have had to pay for the same area of prairie grass or alkali flat.

The homesteader would proceed to clear his land as fast as possible. This was no task for the easily discouraged, for the Redwood was not like the ordinary tree: not only was it a major project to cut one down, but also once felled the damned thing would not stay dead. The stump would at once send up a circle of hopeful shoots (in the virgin groves such circles of trees grown to giants can be seen standing around a charred stump more than a thousand years old.) "All the brains, religion, and superstition of the neighborhood are brought into play to prevent a new growth," wrote John Muir. "The sprouts from the roots and stumps are cut off again and again, with zealous concern as to the best time and method of making death sure. In the clearings of one of the largest mills on the coast we found thirty men at work, last summer, cutting off Redwood shoots 'in the dark of the moon,' claiming that all the stumps and roots cleared at this auspicious time would send up no more shoots."

But with time and enough perseverance, the homesteaders won out. Vineyards near the Russian river, sheep meadows on the Mendocino coast, cow pastures between Scotia and Eureka, on the lower Klamath and near Crescent City, are still sown with the burned-off stumps of hundreds of forest giants, some as large or larger than the biggest trees still standing along the Redwood Highway. "A sense of more than depression confronts the traveller who takes this desolation to heart," writes John A. Crow in *California As a Place to Live.* "It is much the same impression left by the scorched earth found in the wake of a passing army.

"Eureka, which is beautifully situated, and could have been one of the most magnificent ports in the whole world, now lies in the midst of this destruction, a barren fishing and lumbering outpost in a denuded forest country. . . . (There) a few Redwood trees shade the picnic grounds, but the countryside is an ugly wasteland of weeds and marshes. There is nothing here to remind the traveller of those immemorial groves which it took Nature so many centuries to create."

The same laws that were meant to benefit settlers proved a boon to timber speculators and operators, who were able to gain control fraudulently of vast tracts of public land under the commutation provision of the Homestead Act. With Redwood timber averaging 90,000 board feet per acre and lumber selling for about $15 per thousand feet, one acre was grossing the mill about $1,350 for every $1.25 invested—a better than fair return on any investment. The greatest frauds were perpetrated under the Timber and Stone Act of 1878. In one notorious scheme at Eureka, farmers were stopped on their way home, merchants called from their counters and sailors lured from "Coffee Jack's," a boarding house, and brought to the Land Office where land claims were filed for them. A shake shanty, often transportable, would be set up on a man's claim, to represent the "homesteader's" "home." Then the "homestead" changed hands for a few dollars. The ultimate lumber operator often had to pay a fair price for his timber—but this profited nobody but the profiteer. Thus the government—and the American people—allowed the most valuable timber lands in the world to pass into the hands of real or phoney homesteaders, for a song.

But then these were the "heroic" days of lumbering, when the sheer brawn of men and beasts was pitted against the great trees. Swedes, Finns, and Norwegians, Frenchmen and Germans, Englishmen, Scotsmen and Irishmen, graduates of the Maine woods and "Bluenoses" from lower Canada made up the population of the Redwood logging camps, and although they might have had trouble at times understanding each other they all shared the same pride in the depth and cleanness of their axe cuts.

The chopping boss—or "bull buck"—planned the strips to be cut, and a set of choppers might work from a month to three months on one strip. A staging was built around the trunk of a tree above the butt swell and on this the pair of choppers stood. Their equipment included two axes, two eight-foot saws, one twelve-foot saw, two dozen plates, one dozen shims, ten wedges, two sledges, one pair of gun stocks, one plumb bob. This last item was all-important, for with it the choppers determined whether the tree was straight or a "leaner," and if the latter they adjusted their cut so as to make it fall in the right direction (usually uphill), where a "bedding" of smaller trees and branches had been prepared to fill in the low spots and to cushion its fall. It was bad luck to the crew that made the slightest miscalculation, for they could bring hundreds of tons of wood crashing down on their heads. Or the tree could fall afoul of its layout and shatter into fragments; hundreds of dollars' worth of wood would be abandoned on the ground and the loggers would move on to the next tree, all their sweat and toil having gone for nought. Falling a giant Redwood up to 12 feet in diameter with hand axe and cross-cut saw often took as much as three days.

Once felled, the trunk was cut into lengths suitable to the market, and the barkers pried off the bark with long poles. Then it was up to the "jackscrewers" to roll the logs within reach of the bull team crew—a dangerous job as the log would sometimes take an unexpected roll. Teams of bulls or oxen (or sometimes horses) hauled the logs down the skid road to the river-side "dump." A string of logs was joined by chains and dog-hooks, with the heaviest butt, weighing up to 20 tons, in the lead. On this the chain-tender rode, keeping a sharp eye on the water-carrier, often a Chinese, whose duty it was to go between the head log and the rear oxen and wet the skids in the road so the logs would slide more easily. "The six to eight yoke of bulls tugging at the long line of bumping logs is one of the most animated scenes in a lumber camp," an eyewitness wrote. "These brutes are of enormous size, stolidly obedient to the 'Whoa haws' and 'Gees' of the teamsters, and surprisingly quick to get out of the way of a flying log. In a hard pull the faithful creatures fairly get down upon their knees to make it."

At the "dump" or landing the jackscrewers took over once more, rolling the logs into the river. (Another common method of bringing the logs to the river was to send them in a box flume—an exciting sight as each naked bole came smoking down at terrific speed, making a huge splash as it struck the water.) Once in the river the logs remained on the spot until the rainy season when freshets could move them. When the rains came, whether it be midnight or daytime, the log drivers were routed out to rush the log jam down the swollen river. Sluice dams were sometimes built to gather a head of water. When enough water had backed up behind the dams they were "tripped" or broken, and the logs were shot down to the mill in the ensuing flash flood.

This system of floating the logs down streams lasted in Humboldt county until about 1880, when logging railroads generally superseded it. In Mendocino county the log drives lasted much longer. In 1928, 20 million board feet of Redwood were successfully flushed down Big River, and the last dam was tripped as late as 1936. The Mendocino streambanks still show the scouring effect of the log drives. It was in Mendocino, too, that the most picturesque methods were used to ship out the lumber. The rugged coast has few natural harbors, but the lumber schooners worked their way into the small coves or "dog holes," mooring under the high sheer cliffs with the aid of their own anchors or of a make-shift buoy. An apron chute extended from the top of the cliff to the ship's pitching deck, and down this the lumber slid. Or it was lowered on swaying slings suspended from a wire cable, one end of which was anchored to the cliff and the other in the cove or ocean. Sometimes whole logs weighing many tons were swung aboard by this method.

At about the time when steam locomotives, dragging long strings of log-carrying flatcars across vertiginous trestles, became a common sight in the Redwood region, another type of steam engine could be heard chugging in the woods. "In 1881," writes Peattie, "John Dolbeer, a pioneer operator among the Eureka Redwoods, brought out of his blacksmith shop an invention that made the bullwhackers guffaw. It was a sort of donkey engine with a vertical boiler, a horizontal one-cylinder engine, and a big drum on which to wind up the tentacles of steel cable. He made these fast to a gigantic log, then opened up his engine wide. The log came thrashing down the skid road faster than the bullwhackers could cuss an ox, and the smirks died from their faces, for their jobs were gone."

The transition was actually not quite that sudden—the last straining bull team was used in 1914—but the "Dolbeer Donkey" and its more powerful offspring quickly revolutionized logging. More efficient than the slow, plodding oxen, they were also far more destructive. The hauling of logs no longer was confined to the skid roads; the butts came crashing through the forest from every direction, ploughing up the ground, crushing the undergrowth, bulldozing young trees in their path. Even more devastating were the fires set by the loggers. "This Big

Basin country is an example, and I can speak on this matter from personal observation," wrote a resident of the Santa Cruz mountains in 1900. "How often, in the hottest of the summer, have I not wished bad luck to the suffocating smoke that covers our beautiful scenery as with a black pall, day after day, hiding the face of Ben Lomond with an unsightly veil, and increasing the temperature by at least ten degrees. If you ask, 'Where is the fire?—it must be doing a great deal of damage,' the aborigine of the mountains will answer with the utmost indifference, 'Oh, no; they are only burning brush in the Big Basin.' Sounds quite harmless, does it not?

"But the burning away of the underbrush means this: a certain section has been designated, or rather doomed, by the owner, to be cleared; that is, the big trees (Redwoods) are to be felled and made ready for the sawmill. When the mighty monarchs of the forest lie prone at last, the entire bark is stripped from off their trunk. . . . Then the torch is applied some fine dark night, and everything in that section, the birds in their nests, the merry little tree-squirrel, the swift deer and the spotted fawn, the giant ferns and the rare orchids—everything is burned to death. The enormous trunks of the Redwoods, green and full of sap, alone resist the fire-fiend; tops, branches, bark, are all burned to ashes, and madroños, oaks, firs, and young Redwood trees are reduced to cinders and pitiful-looking black stumps."

Such protests were of little avail against an industry which by the turn of the century had become the most important in the State. As the population grew so did its demand for wood—in all of its uses. And such was the versatility of Redwood that its applications were practically unlimited. Dr. W. L. Jepson gave a striking summary of them in his *The Trees of California* (1923): "The writer of these lines is a Californian. He was rocked by a pioneer mother in a cradle made of Redwood. The house in which he lived was largely made of Redwood. His clothing, the books of his juvenile library, the saddle for his riding pony were brought in railway cars chiefly made of Redwood, running on rails laid on Redwood ties, their course controlled by wires strung on Redwood poles. He went to school in a Redwood schoolhouse, sat at a desk made of Redwood and wore shoes the leather of which was tanned in Redwood vats. Everywhere he touched Redwood. Boxes, bins, bats, barns, bridges, bungalows were made of Redwood. Posts, porches, piles, pails, pencils, pillars, paving-blocks, pipe lines . . . were made of Redwood. . . .

"One of the most emphatic tributes to the economic value of Redwood is that new uses are constantly being discovered for it. We ship our choicest grapes to distant lands packed in Redwood sawdust. We replace steel water-conduits with Redwood. We supply Redwood doors to the Central American market because the white ant does not eat Redwood.''

And so, being "too good to live," the Redwoods continued to fall by the thousands every year. The 20th Century brought increasing mechanization to logging operations. Both in the woods and the mills methods became more and more efficient, and less backbreaking to the men. The gasoline-powered chainsaw replaced the old handsaws, and lopped off the trees like a guillotine. In 1935, crawler tractors began to drag the logs to the landings, rendering the donkey engine obsolete. Except where the ground is too steep and "high-lead" logging—cable-hauling the logs up abrupt slopes—is necessary, the "cats" are used almost exclusively today. Huge off-highway trucks generally supplanted the logging railroads in the task of bringing the logs from landing to mill, and dusty logging roads everywhere penetrated the forest, making accessible even the most remote stands.

For the first 30 years of the century, the annual "cut" averaged 500,000,000 board feet of Redwood. During the Depression years of the 'Thirties this dropped to 300,000,000. But in World War II the drain on the forests accelerated. Immense quantities of Redwood timber were rushed to the Pacific theater. Wartime restrictions on home construction and other consumer uses of wood limited the cut. But the demand was there, accumulating like water behind a dam. And with V-J Day the dam burst. The tempo of cutting speeded up and by the early 'Fifties reached 1 billion board feet of Redwood a year. The number of sawmills in the Redwood region (including those sawing Douglas fir and other species) jumped from 117 in 1945 to 299 in 1947 to 398 in 1948. Most of the new mills were small outfits that would log a plot of land and then close down—throughout the Redwood Belt one runs across the rusting ruins of such fly-by-night mills. Too many of them operated on the "cut out and get out" principle—interested only in making a quick profit, the owners cared not how they treated the land, and left it in no condition to reforest itself. Many specialized in so-called "split products"—chopping up thousand-year-old trees into grapestakes and fencing and shingles.

Today, the snarling whine of the chainsaws, the growl of huge "cats" everywhere rend the silence of the woods. Herds of gigantic trucks come thundering down from the hills in clouds of dust, dwarfed by the logs they carry, and jam up the tourist traffic along the Redwood Highway. In the big mills' yards can be seen whole forests of trees—massive "decks" of logs each thicker than a man is tall, rows of towering stacks of rough-cut lumber. Back in the woods the logged-off sections look like Tarawa after the Marines had landed. Where once a carpet of Redwood sorrel and lady fern spread there is nothing but bare earth, churned up by the tractors' treads and strewn with "slash"—tree tops, branches, shattered pieces of trunks and sundry other logging waste. Muddy streams, with beds obstructed by debris, run between denuded banks, sorry reminders of the beautiful clear creeks that once cheered the forest with their music. Great stumps rise from the ground like the tombstones of trees. And the Redwoods left standing to reseed the forest look like caricatures. They soon clothe their nude flanks from butt to crown with fuzzy foliage, almost as if ashamed of their sudden exposure. Seen from the air, logged areas are an intricate maze of tractor trails, like worm tracks under the bark of an infested tree, and the boundaries of state parks are as sharply defined as on a map.

The biggest, most beautiful, and accessible trees are going first. How much longer can this destruction last? Not very long. In 1909, there were an estimated 102 billion board feet of old growth Redwood in the forests; in 1920, 72 billion; in 1931, 57 billion. By 1953, the U.S. Forest Service estimated that the "live sawtimber volume" of Redwood, including some second-growth, was down to 35 billion board feet. And in 1960 the Forest Service predicted that at the current rate of cutting the bulk of virgin Redwood in private hands (and 93 per cent of the old growth is in private hands) would be gone by 1980. The increasing commercial use of Redwood and the expanding population are likely to shorten this estimate. All the inventive talents of the industry, all the promotional talents of the California Redwood Association, are devoted to increasing the use and uses of Redwood, to spurring domestic demand for Redwood products and finding new markets abroad. Heavy taxes on standing timber by counties in the Redwood Belt speed the liquidation of the virgin growth. It matters not to the tax assessor whether the owner wants to log or not: the trees must be converted into dollars. And many an owner of small timber lands—a rancher, for instance, or the proprietor of a resort—who may want to keep his trees finds that he cannot afford to do so, and so he sells his timber to the loggers. Emanuel Fritz, Professor of Forestry Emeritus at the University of California and consulting forester to the California Redwood Association, wrote in April, 1963 to the Save-the-Redwoods League: "I used to think that these groves are safe in the hands of the owners who, for some time, were apparently doing well running resorts for tourists and campers. But this is all changed. High taxes, and increased costs of running a 90-day tourist camp make it impossible to own old-growth Redwoods as an attraction when their competitors have no such expense. As to the taxes, you have here an excellent example of the power of taxation to destroy."

With every proud owner of a new Redwood home, with every suburbanite who repanels his living room with Redwood or beautifies his patio with Redwood planters and furniture, the end of the great trees draws nearer. It takes a Redwood 1000 years or more to mature. Man, armed with chainsaw, can cut it down in an hour. It took Nature over 100 million years to create the world's most sublime forest. Within a few years the remnants of the virgin forest will be gone—destroyed by man in little more than a century.

BURNED SNAG, FORMER HOMESTEAD NEAR SCOTIA

THE HEROIC DAYS

NEAR EUREKA, 1919

Sawmill fodder, Yager Creek

It took brawn—
of men and beasts
and unsophisticated machines—
to take the Redwoods down.

Twenty-two Davids and one Goliath, near Elk River

Log Dump along the Elk River

Bull team and bullwhackers

There was no wood quite like this.
Alive or dead it was made to endure.

Logging train

Remnants of a once giant forest, Klamath Glen

TREE FARM NORTH OF ORICK, 1963

STREAMBEDS ON TREE FARM NEAR ORICK, 1963

LOGGED SLOPE, KLAMATH RIVER, 1963

THE NEW
TECHNOLOGY

LOGGING TRUCK AND REDWOOD LOAD

*With modern chainsaws, cats, and trucks,
man cuts the Redwoods down to size.
A tree that took a millenium to grow
can be felled in less than an hour*

LOG CRANE

HORIZONTAL FOREST, ORICK

"Shelterwood cutting" in the Northern Redwoods Purchase
District Experimental Forest of the U.S. Forest Service.
The only other Federally-owned Redwood land is the small
grove in Muir Woods National Monument.

DENUDED HILLSIDE, STARWEIN RIDGE ON THE KLAMATH

The "Malarkey Forest" near Crescent City, originally preserved as a memorial by the M. & M. Woodworking Co., and cut in the 'fifties when the land changed hands.

JAPANESE FREIGHTER, EUREKA

THE REDWOODS GO TO SEA ...

LOGGING DEBRIS AND DRIFTWOOD, MOUTH OF THE SMITH RIVER

5. CONSERVATION OR PRESERVATION?

"I feel most emphatically that we should not turn into shingles a tree which was old when the first Egyptian conqueror penetrated to the valley of the Euprates, which it has taken so many thousands of years to build up, and which can be put to better use. That you may say is not looking at the matter from the practical standpoint. There is nothing more practical in the end than the preservation of beauty, than the preservation of anything that appeals to the higher emotions in mankind."

In this speech, made 60 years ago, Theodore Roosevelt was talking about the Sierra Big Trees. But he could have said much the same of the Coast Redwoods—except that the oldest of these may date its birth "only" at a century or two before Christ. And yet, of perhaps 1,500,000 acres of Redwoods whose majestic ranks covered northern California's coastal hills and valleys before logging began, only 86,723 acres—and not all of virgin growth—have been set apart in the state parks to "appeal to the higher emotions in mankind." The balance has been dedicated for over a century to the manufacture of shingles and other products of the lumber industry.

And despite the rapidly dwindling reserves of old-growth timber, the liquidation of these reserves continues at an accelerated pace, as if the forests were inexhaustible. Indeed the forests *are* inexhaustible, if properly managed, the argument runs. The major lumber companies in the area, who own or have cutting rights on a large proportion of Redwood timberlands, have a vested interest in staying in business. And so, unlike the "cut out and get out" operators, most of them try to log in such a fashion that their lands will be left in a productive condition. Their goal is "sustained" or "perpetual" yield. And the realization that "conservation" makes economic sense has widened to the point where an increasing number of smaller operators and/or owners of timberlands are trying to manage their holdings so that their first "crop" of Redwood will not be their last.

It took a long time for such an attitude to develop, for loggers to realize—or care—that unless nature were treated with respect it would rebel and refuse to grow anything but brush where Redwoods once had thrived. The donkey engine and cable-yarding method used from 1881 to the 1930s was so destructive that it left cutover lands almost devoid of a seed source. But it was not until 1923 that a systematic program of planting was undertaken. Large nurseries were established and the nursery seedlings were planted by hand on the cutover lands. But seedling mortality was high, especially during the hot summer months. The Depression brought this attempt to an abrupt end.

In the mid-'thirties two related innovations seemed to give the Redwood forest a new lease on life. One was the advent of the crawler tractor, which soon made the donkey engine and wire-cable logging obsolete. Self-propelled and maneuverable, the tractor could in theory skirt young trees and thus avert the wholesale destruction of all plant life which cable logging entailed. At the same time, the "selective logging" principle was first applied to the Redwoods—a principle which in Montana was humorously defined as "You select a forest and you log it." But as described by the lumber companies the "selective logging" theory seems to make sense. A virgin stand of Redwoods is made up of trees of all ages—just as the population of a city includes babies and octogenarians. The older trees—the veterans of a thousand years or more—grow very slowly, and by usurping sunlight and moisture and the nutrients in the soil they slow the growth of the younger trees. From the point of view of a logger, who appraises a forest in "board feet," such a stand is "static" or "overmature." Nature, working by her own methods, has practiced "forest renewal" so successfully that our present Redwoods are the direct, recognizable descendants of trees that thrived in the age of dinosaurs. It has created such marvels as the Rockefeller Forest in Bull Creek Flat. But in a way, it has botched the job: from the "practical" standpoint it would be better to clear out the old trees and give the younger ones a chance to come into their own. For a young Redwood, once released by natural causes or by logging from the tyranny of its elders, is one of the fastest growing of trees.

This rapid early growth, and the peculiar ability of a Redwood once cut to resprout from stump or roots, form the basis of the "selective cutting" rationale. Step Number 1 is to cut down the old giants, leaving the younger trees to grow more rapidly in volume and quantity, to provide seed for natural regeneration, to shade the ground against too-rapid desiccation during the dry summers and to protect the soil against erosion. From the stumps of the old trees new sprouts will shoot up. Step Number 2, some years later, is to log off the "release growth" of younger trees which by then will have attained merchantable proportions. The seedlings which these will have sowed and the stump sprouts from the original growth will be "harvested" at Step Number 3 of the cycle. And so on in perpetuity.

Guard against fire, except for controlled burning of slash, take a few precautions to minimize soil erosion, leave a few trees standing to provide seed for regeneration, and in theory the Redwoods can be harvested periodically like any other crop, like alfalfa or cotton or black-eyed peas. "Visitors to the area sometimes express concern over appearance of the land immediately after logging," a major Redwood logging company's brochure concedes. "It takes big equipment to move the heavy logs over steep country. The ground does get scuffed. Like a corn field just after the harvest, it presents a ruffled picture. But people are not alarmed at the appearance of a corn field because they know that next year a new crop will stand in its place. We call our forest lands TREE FARMS, but we plan to take many years between harvests. When the time has passed, the land will be full again, just like the corn field will be next year."

In 1950, 16 years after the introduction of "selective cutting" to the Redwood region, the first Redwood "tree farm" was certified. Since then 644,966 acres of Redwood timberlands have been designated as "tree farms." In a way, the certification of a "tree farm" is like the ordination of a priest or the admittance of a lawyer to the bar: It is the industry itself which, through the California Redwood Association, decides what standards of forestry are required on a tree farm and whether an individual operation meets these standards or not. The basic principles for eligibility to become a "Tree Farmer" are: 1. To assure the California Redwood Association of willingness to maintain the land designated as a "tree farm" in a condition to produce forest crops under good forest practices; 2. To provide reasonable protection from fire and other damage, including excessive grazing; 3. To harvest the crop of standing timber on the "tree farm" in a manner which will assure further crops; and 4. To furnish information concerning his "tree farm" when requested to do so by the California Redwood Association, such information to embrace progress, future plans, improvements, protection, and cutting practices. But whereas an errant priest can be defrocked or a lawyer disbarred, a logger who fails to observe minimum sound logging practices cannot be prevented from operating by his peers. The "tree farm" movement is self-policing, but the "policeman" has no handcuffs.

Yet self-regulation by the industry is the only practical form of regulation in effect at present. The Forest Practice Act, passed by the California Legislature in 1946 and since amended, has the stated purpose "to conserve and maintain the productivity of the timberlands in the interest of the economic welfare of the state and the continuance of the forest industry; to establish . . . standards of forest practice . . . adopted to promote the maximum sustained productivity of the forest. . . ." Pursuant to the Act, rules were established requiring certain minimum measures for "fire prevention and control, for protection against timber operations which unnecessarily destroy young timber growth or timber productivity of the soil, for prevention and control of damage by forest insects, pests and disease, and measures for the restocking of the land." The Act requires timber owners to file cutting plans with the State Forester and loggers to obtain permits from him before commencing timber operations, and specifies penalties for violations of the rules.

How effective has the Forest Practice Act been? Not very. As far as erosion control is concerned, the Act has provided no comprehensive standards or guidelines for judging whether there has been compliance with the law. The word "erosion" is not used at all in the language of the Act itself. Presumably, the individual rule-making committees were left to figure out for themselves what forces cause erosion. As a result, the committees have foundered. One set of rules enjoins the operator to "take all reasonable steps . . . to maintain the productivity of timberlands in his logging area and . . . (to exercise) due diligence . . . to prevent . . . washout or gullying. . . ." But what are "all reasonable steps"? What is "due diligence"? Would a Vehicle Code which merely admonished drivers to "be careful" and to "exercise due diligence" be adequate? The result has been that sloppy practices have passed for compliance with the admittedly minimum regulations the law provides. Furthermore, although the Act divides the state into four different forest practice districts and provides for different practice rules in each, on the basic premise that varying terrain, soil stability and chemistry, and differences in native vegetation should all be taken into account before writing rules to prevent erosion, little has been done to follow through on this premise. Though forest conditions vary as widely within each district as between any two districts, each district has only a single blanket set of rules. Dr. Paul Zinke, Assistant Professor of Forestry at the University of California School of Forestry, has pointed out that "a uniform set of practices formulated for such a wide variety of landscape conditions is bound to result in a failure under some of these conditions." And since the practice rules are recognized as *minimum regulations,* it is logical to conclude that they do not meet the erosion problem under most conditions.

If the rules are inadequate, the enforcement provisions are even more so. The Legislature up to now has budgeted for only eight regular inspectors to canvass the entire state of California. As a result, the average operator is visited slightly more than once a year for inspection of his operations under the Forest Practice Act, and the average operation even less frequently, since most logging companies have many operations. This is equivalent to cutting down the Highway Patrol to the point where the average driver would see a patrolman on the highway only once a year. The Legislature has no such faith in the capacity of the average motorist for self-regulation. Should it have greater faith in the standards of the average logger? More than 1,500 violations of the Forest Practice Act and related laws are discovered every year, according to the most conservative figures. Yet it was not until 1962—16 years after the Act was passed—that the first three complaints were sustained in court. The Office of the Attorney General, charged with the duty of prosecuting Forest Practice Act violations, apparently had taken its responsibilities lightly. Of more than 25,000 violations subsequent to 1946 the Attorney General's office had obtained only three convictions. Whether this was due to incompetence or lack of interest—either could spell disaster for California's future forests.

Finally, the Act contains a major loophole. Upon the simple affidavit of the timberland owner stating a "bona fide" intention to put the land to other use, the owner may chop down every tree on his property regardless of the suitability of his land for the substituted use, or the erosion which results. Not only has erosion often ruined the land converted, but it has frequently damaged adjoining property and property lower on the same watershed. And, according to a 1956 report of the Division of Forestry, "There is some feeling that people who do not wish to observe the Forest Practices Rules have found it convenient to utilize certain exemptions provided (by this loophole) to escape compliance with the rules without carrying out the intent of devoting the land to other than timber-growing use."

As far as erosion control is concerned, the effectiveness of present logging practices and of the Forest Practices Rules can be gauged by some figures released by the United States Forest and Range Experiment Station in Berkeley. The current annual levels of soil losses from some north coast drainages, measured in tons of sediment per square mile of drainage, reach 8,950 tons on the South Fork of the Eel; 5,300 on the Van Duzen; 4,800 on the Eel River at Scotia; 3,120 on the Mad River. Where it runs through extensive National Forest lands, the Mad River still is fairly clear, with a loss of only 329 tons per square mile. The loss from the South Fork of the Eel amounts to 6 pounds of soil for every square yard of land, floated out to sea every year. And while logging is not the sole cause of these erosion losses, it is the prime cause.

Obviously, our Redwood logging companies are going to have to exhibit greater care and respect for their lands if these are not in time to become barren wastes incapable of supporting Redwoods or anything else. Standards will need to be a good deal higher and enforcement much stricter if "tree farming" and "sustained yield" are to be more than public relations slogans. And one begins to be somewhat skeptical of such statements as that once made by Professor Fritz, that "the future of the Redwood forests has never been more secure." To be sure, there are areas which were logged long ago and where there are now fine stands of second-growth Redwood. In other areas, however, the quality of the second-growth Redwood has proved so disappointing that owners have turned to clear cutting the Redwood, bulldozing the land, and reseeding with Douglas fir. Immediately south of Prairie Creek Redwoods State Park, Highway 101 traverses a scene of apocalyptic devastation, where not a tree was left standing. But big signs along the road try to reassure the passing public: "14,000,000 seeds planted on 200 tree farm acres," they read. And at a road-side pavilion the traveller can view samples of Redwood siding and panelling, and can pick up pamphlets titled "Forest Renewal Story." What neither signs nor pamphlets mention is that the company has reseeded *not with Redwood* but with Douglas fir, spruce and cedar.

It would be unfair at this time, only 13 years after the first "tree farm" was certified in the Redwood region, to dismiss the goal of "perpetual yield" as a mirage, or to suggest that "tree farms" are just a public relations device. But by the same token one may validly question whether a few decades' experience with "sustained yield" practices is sufficient to justify industry predictions that once the virgin Redwood stands are liquidated the lumber interests "will have continuing supplies of (second growth) forests for maintaining a steady flow of products to the home-builders and industries." Indeed one may legitimately wonder whether Redwoods can really be "harvested" like any other "crop," whether "tree farm" is an apt term for a logging operation no matter how "scientific."

Under natural conditions, a Redwood forest may take

from 500 to 1,000 years to replace itself. Yet the companies plan to shorten the renewal cycle to 50 years or so. In a virgin forest, the total mass of organic matter—of living trees and other plants, of decomposing wood and foliage—remains more or less constant, in a continuous cycle of life and growth and death and decay. But when loggers "harvest" the forest and remove the wood they have cut, there is a net loss to the forest of organic matter. In real farming, farmers compensate for this loss by fertilizing their fields. "Tree farmers" do nothing of the kind. It might be more accurate to describe their operations as "tree mining," since in a very real sense loggers mine the organic wealth of the forests. They have a boundless faith in Nature's ability to heal its wounds—and to continue doing so every half century. But does a "second growth" not represent a stretching of the membrane of life? Will a "third growth" and "fourth growth" and "fifth growth" stretch the membrane increasingly thin— to the point where eventually it must tear? Is there no danger that the periodic mining of the forest's organic wealth and the repeated disturbance of its soil (with the resulting erosion) will in the end lead to the total exhaustion of the land?

At our present level of knowledge such questions have no answers. "We know next to nothing about forest soils," admitted Bernard Frank when he was assistant chief of the U.S. Forest Service. The bulk of the Redwood being cut is still virgin growth, and not until several forest generations have been grown and logged, not until fifth- and sixth-growth trees are being sawed at the mills will we know if "sustained yield" can really be sustained. If we were really as scientific as we pretend to be, and really cared about the perpetuation of our Redwoods, we should probably halt all logging except on experimental stands, where different methods of "clear" or "selective" cutting could be tried and evaluated over a number of logging and growing cycles. Only then, if the results justified it, would large-scale logging be resumed, just as a new surgical technique wins general adoption only after it has been thoroughly tested first on laboratory animals and then on "hopeless" human subjects. But the public demands Redwood products, the industry has a big investment in plants and equipment, the counties of the Redwood region depend largely on timber taxes—and so the public will continue to buy Redwood homes, the industry to reap its profits and the counties to collect their taxes even at the risk of ultimate deforestation—the very process which turned the Middle East, once a "land of milk and honey," into a barren and desert land.

The most we can hope for is that "conservation" measures practiced by the best in the industry will be adopted by *all*, that continued refinements in the mills will further reduce wastage—a saving at the mills that means a saving of trees—and that Nature will play along with the loggers by growing as much Redwood as they can cut. But "conservation" is a word that has two meanings in the Redwood area. One is economic conservation —the kind with which the lumber companies are concerned. The other is aesthetic. It is the kind of conservation that seeks to preserve the virgin Redwoods in their natural state, as the world's finest forest, as a unique treasure which once lost can never be regained. "Preserving" the Redwoods has nothing to do with the success or failure of the "sustained yield" experiment. For no matter how vigorous, a second-growth Redwood forest aesthetically is a second-rate Redwood forest. There is nothing inspirational about a stand of slim young Redwoods with an arbitrarily-set life expectancy of 50 years or so. There is nothing unique about them, either. They have a beauty of their own, to be sure—but so do young evergreens everywhere. They will never match the majesty, the mystery, the primeval beauty of the virgin Redwoods, for they will not be given the chance to do so. If these qualities are worth preserving for themselves, if, as Teddy Roosevelt said, "there is nothing more practical in the end than the preservation of beauty," then the highest form of conservation is the maintenance in their natural state of as many of our virgin Redwoods as possible.

Bald Ridge, and likely to remain bald

FOREST RENEWAL

Selective cutting near Prairie Creek Redwoods State Park—
"seed trees" and "release growth" where a giant forest
once stood

Tree farm near Orick
"14 Million Seeds Planted"—but not of Redwood.

14 MILLION SEEDS
PLANTED
ON 200 TREE FARM ACRES
LOGGED 1961   SEEDED 1962
ARCATA REDWOOD COMPANY
EXHIBIT 1 MILE NORTH ON RIGHT

"Forest Renewal Exhibit" near Orick
"The ground does get scuffed . . . It presents a ruffled
picture." (Arcata Redwood Company brochure.)

Ah Pak Creek on the Klamath
    A muddy effluent, obstructed by debris from denuded banks,
flows where clear streams once cheered the forest with
    their music.

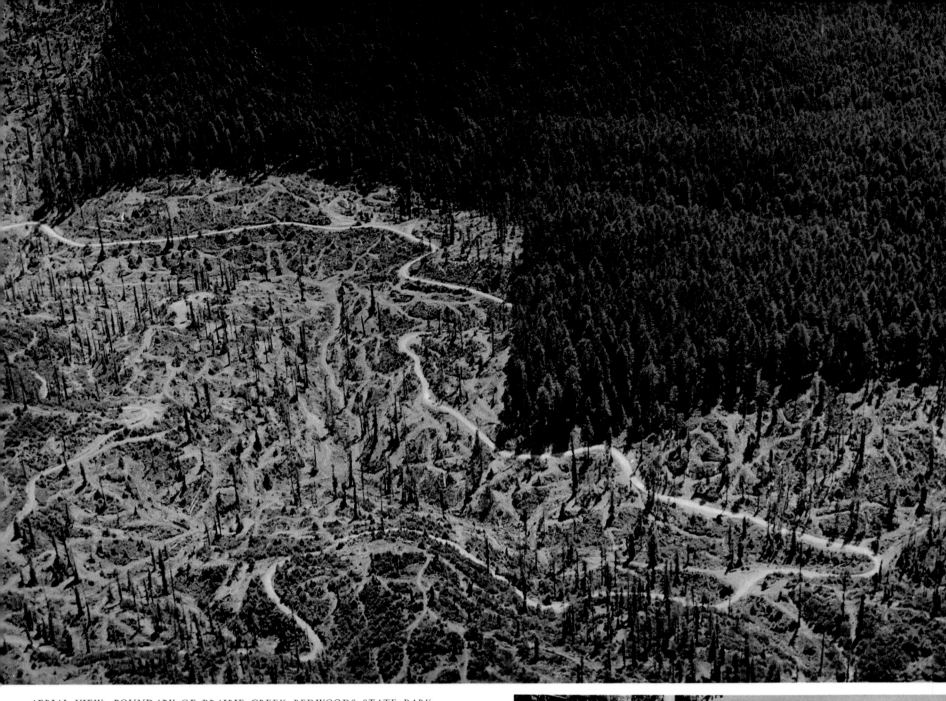

AERIAL VIEW, BOUNDARY OF PRAIRIE CREEK REDWOODS STATE PARK

AND FOREST PRESERVATION

From the air, logged areas are a maze of tractor trails, and the actual boundaries of state parks are as sharp as the line on the map.

GROUND VIEW, EDGE OF PRAIRIE CREEK REDWOODS STATE PARK

REDWOOD HIGHWAY, 1913

BIG LEAF MAPLES AND REDWOOD, PRAIRIE CREEK REDWOODS STATE PARK

STREAM IN PEPPERWOOD FLAT

PRAIRIE CREEK, PRAIRIE CREEK REDWOODS STATE PARK

BULL CREEK FLAT

6. "SAVING" THE REDWOODS

"Any fool can destroy trees," John Muir once wrote. "They cannot run away; and if they could they would still be destroyed—chased and hunted down as long as fun or a dollar could be got out of their bark hides, branching horns, or magnificent bole backbones. . . . God has cared for these (Sequoias), saved them from drought, disease, avalanches, and a thousand straining, leveling tempests and floods; but he cannot save them from fools—only Uncle Sam can do that."

Spurred on by conservationists, Uncle Sam early came to the rescue of the Sierra Big Trees. Yosemite, ceded to California in 1864 to be a park for all the nation, became a national park *per se* in 1890. In that same year Sequoia National Park and the General Grant grove were preserved by federal acts. Today, close to 97 per cent of the virgin stand of *Sequoia gigantea* is protected in national parks, national forests, or state parks. (Outside these reserves there is still sporadic cutting of these magnificent trees, despite their unsuitability as timber, and operators try to pass off the lumber as "Redwood.")

But Uncle Sam took no such interest in the Coast Redwoods. In 1900 not one of these trees enjoyed public protection: on every Redwood alive the logging season was permanently open. Luckily there were men and women who found this scandalous, and in May 1900 they formed the Sempervirens Club of California and began to campaign for the establishment of a public park in the coastal Redwoods. They did their work well: prominent citizens throughout the State rallied to the cause, as did important scientific bodies in the eastern states and other localities outside California, and in 1902 the Legislature approved a bill appropriating $250,000 for the purchase of 3,800 acres of Redwoods in Big Basin, in the Santa Cruz mountains. Five years later, Congressman William Kent snapped up 295 acres of Redwoods sheltered in a canyon at the southwest base of Mount Tamalpais just ahead of a water company which wanted to flood the canyon. And the next year Kent gave his purchase to the people of the United States in honor of his friend John Muir, and President Theodore Roosevelt accepted it under authority of the Antiquities Act. Today Muir Woods National Monument, expanded to 510 acres by a further gift from Kent, is the most visited Redwood grove, standing as it does less than an hour's drive north of San Francisco.

These two groves, another protected by Santa Cruz county, a small tract owned by Sonoma county and another by the Bohemian Club, were the only Redwoods preserved from the loggers' saws when the United States entered World War I. At that time, a new threat developed to the northern Redwoods. The State decided to rebuild the highway running north from San Francisco to the Oregon border. The new road would give lumbermen easier access to the finest stands of all, and it seemed a fair bet that the Humboldt and Del Norte Redwoods would shortly be falling like grain before the scythe. In the summer of 1917 three prominent conservationists—Henry Fairfield Osborn, president of the American Museum of Natural History; John C. Merriam, then professor of paleontology at the University of California and afterward for 18 years president of the Carnegie Institution of Washington; and Madison Grant, an amateur scientist and president of the New York Zoological Society—took a sightseeing trip through the Humboldt Redwoods. And what they saw appalled them. As Dr. Osborn described it, "There are parts of the northwestern highways where for miles the road is narrowed and blocked with piled grape stakes and shingles, and on either hand the ground is covered with a jumble of treetops, branches, slabs and bark, which should have gone into the manufacture of some by-product.

"But," he added, "also there are stretches where the roadway leads from open sunshine and distant views of green, wooded mountain slopes into the giant forest and on through colonnades of trees where the air is cool and fragrant and long beams of sunlight slant down through the green of Redwood foliage." The three men returned from the northern woods determined that some, at least, of the "colonnades" would remain vertical. And they wasted no time in setting up an organization and a plan of action. Early in 1918 they founded the Save-the-Redwoods League, which at once began to collect members and funds—and publicity for its cause. Articles by Osborn and Grant in the *National Geographic* and by Albert Atwood, Joseph Hergesheimer, and Samuel G. Blythe in the *Saturday Evening Post* began to awaken the American public to the impending fate of the Redwoods and brought in a flood of two-dollar contributions to the League. These supplemented the large donations of such men as Stephen

Mather, Director of the National Park Service, William Kent, and John Phillips of Wenham, Massachusetts, whose gift went for a memorial grove to Colonel Raynal C. Bolling, the first American officer of the upper ranks to be killed in action in World War I.

By 1920, when the League was incorporated as a non-profit corporation, its membership had topped four thousand, and it had bought four pieces of Redwood land along the highway in Humboldt County. Its basic objectives were set: to purchase for a state park the best Redwood acreage obtainable along the northern highway, and to preserve as broad a spread of Redwood forest as possible, ideally as a national park. The national park objective was never realized—Uncle Sam never became that interested in the Coast Redwoods. But if Washington wouldn't help, perhaps Sacramento would. In 1921, the League threw its weight behind a proposal for a $300,000 appropriation to purchase Redwood lands. As Robert Shankland described it in his biography, *Steve Mather of the National Parks,* "Under urging, committees from the upper and lower houses (of the Legislature) met in joint session. Forceful arguments then unfurled from a throng of persuasive Californians. The joint committee succumbed without much of a struggle and sponsored a bill for $300,000. Word soon circulated, however, that the Governor, William D. Stephens, was staring at it doubtfully, and the Governor received a visit from the same contingent that had tackled the legislative committee. He said that he could not guarantee approval: the State was poor, the schools were inadequate, and so on. One of the petitioners, William Kent, who had been in Congress with him, leaped to his feet. 'Hell, Bill,' he said, 'shut the schools down. The kids would enjoy it, and it would only take them a year or two to make the work up. If these trees all go, it will take two thousand years to make *them* up.' The Governor signed."

Further success attended the Save-the-Redwoods League's legislative efforts in 1927 when the Legislature set up the State Park Commission and directed it to make a survey of potential state park areas—a survey which was entrusted to the noted landscape architect Frederick Law Olmsted; and in 1928 when the State voted a six million dollar bond issue so that private contributions for the purchase of park lands would be matched by the State on a dollar-for-dollar basis. In promoting the bond issue, the League was joined by the California Redwood Association and the National Lumber Manufacturers Association—which was symbolic of the generally harmonious relationships the League had succeeded in establishing with the lumber industry with which it dealt.

From the start, the League operated on the principle that the best way to attain its objectives was not to tackle the Redwood industry as an enemy, but rather to enlist its cooperation through friendly negotiations. The League's aim was not to save *all* the Redwoods and put the companies out of business, but to preserve enough of the virgin stands so that their perpetuation could be assured and the generations of the future could enjoy their unparalleled beauty. By keeping its objectives limited—and then working patiently but persistently to attain them—the League enhanced its chances of success. And by accepting the premise that the Redwood industry should be interfered with to the least extent compatible with the public good, and by standing for fair compensation to those owners whose properties were desired for park purposes, the League won the respect and confidence of the timber operators.

This is not to say that the League's job was easy, or that the lumber people were always altruistic in making the desired lands available. As the League's Secretary, former National Parks Director Newton B. Drury, wrote recently, ". . . for 45 years the League has been operating just a jump ahead of the sawmills as far as money-raising and land acquisition are concerned, and the State has been limited in appropriated funds that could be applied to land planning." Sometimes the knowledge that the League was interested in a given section of land merely spurred the owner to log it off. Today, state park holdings in the Redwood country are almost everywhere hedged in by logging right up to their edges, in what looks suspiciously like a calculated plan to block the parks' future expansion. On the other hand, there have been numerous instances where lumber operators have held off cutting portions of their land wanted by the League, and have been generous in giving the League time to raise the purchase funds (while *they* raised the price). At the present time, the Simpson Redwood Company is refraining from logging some of its lands adjacent to Jedediah Smith State Park, and The Pacific Lumber Company is reserving from the chain-saws some magnificent stands in the Pepperwood flats which are desired for an extension of the Avenue of the Giants (both these tracts are generally assumed by the motorist who drives through them to be already a part of the parks).

In its 45 years, the Save-the-Redwoods League has succeeded in acquiring and has helped save as state parks 75,000 acres in the Redwood belt, including some of the finest virgin stands, with the understanding that the State will "preserve their naturalness, enhance their beauty and, increase their usefulness and inspiration to nature-lovers all over the world." To buy these lands the League raised over $10,000,000, most of which was matched by the State. It is estimated that it would cost $250,000,000 to purchase the same tracts at today's inflated prices. The League's present master plan aims at the eventual preservation of 125,000 acres of Redwoods, or less than 10 per cent of the original stand, which seems moderate enough when one considers that had it been possible to save *all* the Redwoods the area thus preserved would still have been less than half the size of New York State's Adirondack Park.

Included in the total acreage now in Redwood state parks are numerous smaller groves, many of them of first quality, in Monterey, Santa Cruz, San Mateo, Marin, Sonoma, Mendocino and Humboldt counties. These range in size from 12 acres in Mendocino's Paul M. Dimmick Memorial Grove, through Richardson Grove's 790 acres in Humboldt county to Samuel H. Taylor State Park's 2,576 acres in Marin county. (Only a small part of the latter includes Redwoods.) The five principal Redwood parks are the Big Basin Redwoods (expanded to 11,521 acres from the first Redwood park established in the Santa Cruz mountains in 1902); the Humboldt Redwoods State Park (36,500 acres); the Prairie Creek Redwoods State Park on the Humboldt-Del Norte county line (10,286 acres); and the Del Norte Coast Redwoods (5,932 acres) and the Jedediah Smith Redwoods State Park (9,532 acres) in Del Norte county.

Each of the Redwood parks has a character of its own. Humboldt Redwoods includes a series of memorial groves along the Redwood Highway, among them the superb Franklin K. Lane Memorial Grove, the Bolling Memorial Grove, and others honoring the memory of a prominent individual. Then there is the Children's Forest, most gifts to which have been made in memory of children who have died; this grove is a fairyland of trees and ferns, meadows and streams, paths and bridges that would enchant any child. Also in Humboldt Redwoods State Park are several larger tracts of virgin Redwoods in which the 300-foot colossi form pure stands. These are the "cathedral groves" *par excellence*; this is the climax forest to dwarf all other climax forests. Along Canoe Creek stands the grove named for the Garden Club of America, which, along with the Native Daughters of the Golden West and the California Federation of Women's Clubs, has been among the Save-the-Redwoods League's most generous contributors. Facing each other across the freeway and the South Fork of the Eel, near its confluence with the main Eel River, are the Dyerville Flat, a stand of unusually tall trees including the "Founders' Tree,"

and, possibly the most sublime of them all, Bull Creek Flat, preservation of which was made possible through the gift by John D. Rockefeller, Jr., of $1,000,000 outright and a second $1,000,000 to match other private gifts. Finally, running through the Humboldt Redwoods is that incomparable stretch of two-lane highway, the "Avenue of the Giants." The road tunnels through the soaring trees, and is best driven, slowly and reverently, in an open-top car.

The Prairie Creek Redwoods, as a Save-the-Redwoods League report describes them, differ "widely in character from that of the Redwood forest of southern Humboldt county with its heavy 'flats' of virgin Redwoods along the river bottoms. The Prairie Creek forest combines both the 'flat' type with the 'slope' type, affording splendid examples of both. The 'slope' timber is unusual in quality, size, and density of stand, and the forest cover very luxuriant. Numerous varieties of ferns, notably the great sword ferns and the delicate lomaria, grow in almost tropical abandon, and rhododendron, huckleberry, and other shrubs. . . . The clover-like oxalis thickly carpets the forest floor and in spring is richly embroidered with patches of wild iris, purple and yellow violets, delicate white trilliums, and redwood lilies. In late May the deep rose rhododendron bursts into its rich flamboyant bloom. In the midst of the woods are many venerable Western maples, the branches and trunks of which are entirely moss covered. The silver fir, a symmetrical and beautiful conifer, is found here. . . ." And so is one of the last surviving herds in California of the Roosevelt elk, a large and handsome member of the deer family, which can often be seen grazing in the broad prairie just south of the park headquarters. The park also includes breathtaking sections of wild ocean beach, backed by the abrupt, 250-foot high Gold Bluffs—one of the finest unspoiled stretches of seashore in the country. If the Save-the-Redwoods League succeeds in its plans, the whole length of beach and bluffs will be added to the park, and with them idyllic Fern Canyon, the perpendicular walls of which are completely tapestried with fronds of five-finger fern.

Farther north, Del Norte Coast Redwoods State Park also adjoins the ocean, and offers spectacular views of surf and rocks. Here the Redwoods grow on slopes right down to the ocean shore, and the understory of rhododendrons is especially flamboyant. Still farther up, near Crescent City, lies Jedediah Smith Redwoods State Park, named after the first white man to lead an expedition to the Pacific through this northwestern corner of California. To many, "Jed Smith" is the most beautiful of all the Redwood parks. Containing one of the most heavily timbered tracts in the world, it includes the National Tribute Grove, honoring the men and women who served in the U.S. armed forces in World War II, and the Frank D. Stout Memorial Grove at the confluence of the Smith River and Mill Creek. Without question, Mill Creek is one of the most exquisite streams in all the Redwood region. The old Crescent City-Grants Pass stagecoach road winds its unhurried way through some of the finest portions of the reserve, which is also traversed by the Redwood Highway. But the traveller along the highway is apt to be lulled into a false sense of complacency by the unscarred beauty of the forest through which he is driving. For between sections within the park—and with no signs to indicate the transitions—the highway crosses a tract of private timberland which extends north to the Smith River. As beautiful as the park lands themselves, this tract so far has escaped the chainsaw. But there is no guarantee that it will continue to be spared, and its acquisition is a prime objective of the Save-the-Redwoods League.

These, then, are the Redwoods that were "saved," reprieved from the axe and the mindless demands of the "market." Ably administered, with an eye to the preservation of their unique natural qualities, by the California State Division of Beaches and Parks, these virgin groves stand in mute tribute to the foresight and tenacity of the Save-the-Redwoods League, without which most of them would have been reduced to stumps and sawlogs. They also stand in tribute to the people of the State of California and to their representatives in Sacramento, who allocated tax monies for the preservation of these trees. They stand, too, as eloquent monuments to the aesthetic sense of tens of thousands of Americans who contributed to their preservation out of the conviction that such a treasure must be "saved for all time." And as Peattie observed, "It is moving, as one travels through the flickering light and shade of the Redwood Highway, to realize that many of these groves were given, in part at least, by people who have never seen the Redwoods and perhaps do not expect ever to see them. For the members of some of the sponsoring organizations live in Iowa or Vermont, in Georgia or New York. The great majority of them are probably not persons of wealth at all. They gave anonymously, they gave purely, they gave to the future, to people yet unborn; they gave not only to the country but to the world. And they gave out of a deep religious feeling that the beauty and age and greatness that here have risen from the earth to tower above us are holy and shall not be profaned."

7. HOW SAFE ARE THE "SAVED"?

One phrase recurs like a leitmotif in almost every book or article that mentions the Redwood state parks. These trees, the writers like to say, have been "preserved for all time." It is a pleasant thought, a comforting thought. One feels he need worry no longer about the fate of these ancient Redwoods. And it is certainly with the assumption that once saved from the woodsman's axe the trees *would* be "preserved for all time" that thousands of Americans have contributed towards their purchase. Tragically, their faith has been betrayed. Directly or indirectly, we have caused many of these great trees to be *lost* for all time. And many more stand on the brink of destruction.

The tragedy of Bull Creek is an object lesson and a warning of what may yet befall other Redwoods whose perpetual preservation is usually taken for granted. Bull Creek Basin is a watershed some 41 square miles, or 26,000 acres, in area, which rises from 130 feet to 3,400 at its highest ridge. Its canyons are deep-cleft, its slopes steep. Its thin soils, derived primarily from Franciscan sediments dating from the late Jurassic or early Upper Cretaceous period, are weak and susceptible to erosion. Heavy rains drench the basin every winter. And yet, over the eons, Nature had succeeded in establishing a perfect balance between the forces of rainfall and drought, of fire and erosion, of life and growth. The chaparral forests on the ridge tops, the Douglas firs of the upper slopes, the mixed Douglas fir and Redwood of the middle slopes and upper canyons, and the pure Coast Redwood forests of the flats all lived in harmony with each other and their environment. Their roots anchored the slopes and drained the subsoil. Clear and unsullied, the creeks tumbled from the canyons and widened into placid streams that meandered through the flatlands, their banks graced by maples and alder, dogwoods and willows. Salmon thrashed their waters and spawned in the gravels, and in the spring the young would gather strength for their swim to the ocean.

"To be sure, erosion did occur," wrote James P. Tryner, an officer of the California Division of Beaches and Parks. "But its scars were minimized and quickly healed by the growth of plant life, so that, at any given time, the over-all aspect of the landscape was one of stability, of permanence and of beauty. Fires were not unknown in the basin, but when they did occur, there was little surface disturbance of the soil, so that the accelerated erosion which followed found no artificial scars in which to work, and so that the materials which were carried away were largely from the upper layers of the earth, leaving the basic structures of the soils intact to encourage and support returning vegetation.

"Surely, major floods did occur, and indeed, evidence found in the flats below shows that 18 seasons of excessively heavy run-off were experienced in the period between the years 1058 and 1958; an average of one flood every 50 years. But were these periodic floods accompanied by corresponding periods of loss and destruction in the forest? Apparently not, for the evidence shows that immediately following each flood the forests in the flats experienced a period of accelerated growth, apparently brought on by the deposition of silt eroded from the top soil levels of the upper basin."

The entire basin, then, formed an ecological unity, and all its components—the trees, the streams, the climate and soil—were interrelated and interdependent. The incomparable forest in Bull Creek Flat, known today as the Rockefeller Forest, did not owe its splendor to factors existing in the flats alone, but was the end product, the climactic achievement of forces at work in the watershed as a whole. Alas this was realized too late. The preservation of Bull Creek Flat became one of the very earliest objectives of the Save-the-Redwoods League, and with the help of John D. Rockefeller, Jr., was achieved in 1931. But only the choicest area was bought—9400 acres in the flats and on the immediately adjacent slopes. The rest of Bull Creek Basin remained in private hands. In 1947, large-scale logging began in the Bull Creek watershed. And this was logging that ranked with the worst, perpetrated by typical "cut out and get out" operators with no care or understanding of the land. These loggers stripped the steep slopes, gutted the canyons, gouged the hills with skid trails and roads. The soil, denuded of its protective trees, reverted to its basic instability, and became easy prey to the winter downpours. The sparkling streams grew dull and muddy; they burst their banks and spread ever wider. Soon the salmon and steelhead were gone from Bull Creek. And still the logging proceeded, unnoticed by the public. By 1954 more than half of the watershed had been laid bare. And between 1950 and 1955, fires completed the devastation of some 7000 acres.

In a few short years, man, in his blind and greedy compulsion to turn trees into dollars, had brutally upset the delicate balance which Nature had built up over the ages. Then in December, 1955, torrential rains fell on the Bull Creek watershed, and the tragic damage that man had done became immediately apparent. In the upper basin, vast slides dumped millions of yards of rock and gravel into the streams, to be carried down towards the flats below. Stream banks were eroded at the base and slid into the creeks. These became roaring torrents flowing on broad expanses of raw gravel. In the period of a few hours, raging waters ripped through the Rockefeller Forest, toppling more than 300 major trees (trees in excess of four feet in diameter, breast high) into Bull Creek's channel, and washing away 50 acres of land from the flats themselves. Debris and logs piled up in the creek channel, until at one point there was a log jam 40 feet high, which completely choked the stream. Protective vegetation was torn from the banks, and an additional 99 trees were undercut so badly that later they had to be felled before clean-up work in the creek could begin. Enormous quantities of debris, silt and gravel were deposited in the flats at the base of the trees, and these deposits, unlike the naturally-occurring accumulations of silt of ages past, were not beneficial but led to the later death of many trees.

The damage was not confined to that one great storm of the winter 1955-56. Every rainy season since then the toll of trees has grown, so that by now well over 500 giant Redwoods have fallen. The undercutting of the banks has continued, and the spreading of the gravel which strangles the plant life along the streams. Bull Creek is no longer the beautiful stream it once was. Where it flows through the flats, it has been widened by erosion from an original width of 50 to 100 feet to widths approaching 300 feet in many places, and the huge quantities of raw gravel deposited in it have raised the level of its bed an estimated five feet.

The Division of Beaches and Parks is scrambling to protect the Rockefeller Forest from further damage. Bulldozers are at work in the streambed of Bull Creek, deepening the channel through the gravel. Dump trucks drive up and spill their load of rocks down the raw banks to halt the undercutting action of the stream. A system of checkdams is planned in the upper basin to arrest the movement of gravel downstream. Above all, it was realized that as long as a large part of the watershed remained in private hands the "protection" enjoyed by the state park lands was illusory, and the Save-the-Redwoods League has been buying up the private holdings and deeding them over to the State in a program of acquisition now more than two-thirds completed. Treated as an ecological unity, protected from fire and logging, helped where necessary by artificial re-vegetation and channel control work, the Bull Creek Basin will in time heal itself. But the trees that were toppled are gone and Bull Creek will not recover its full beauty.

If the Bull Creek tragedy has taught us anything, it is the necessity to consider the whole ecological setting of any area which we may desire to preserve in its natural condition. Particularly is this true in the Redwood region with its heavy precipitation and unstable soils. The Redwood parks are not islands, and they can and will be damaged by logging and fires and other destruction occurring beyond their boundaries but within the same watersheds. The parks, to be really protected, must include *whole watersheds*, and this is not the case at present. Jedediah Smith, for instance, includes only the lower portion of Mill Creek. Most of the stream's watershed is still in private hands, and a big new sawmill has been erected upstream from the park. Here the terrain is not as steep as in Bull Creek Basin, and hopefully the loggers will be more cautious in their operations. But the rainfall is even heavier than in Humboldt county. At the very least, we may expect that upstream logging will soil Mill Creek's pristine beauty, (some muddying already has been reported). At worst, Mill Creek could become worse than Bull Creek.

The implications of the Bull Creek lesson are of nation-wide importance. The need to preserve a region's ecological integrity applies just as well to the Grand Canyon or the Everglades. And the Bull Creek experience has ethical and legal aspects that transcend the Redwoods. Who was primarily hurt by the loggers' and timber owners' rape of the Bull Creek Basin? Not the loggers and the timber owners but the owners of the Rockefeller Forest—i.e. the people of the State of California. Who is paying to repair the devastated land? Again, not the loggers and the timber owners who ruined it, but the people of California. "Under our present criminal code," writes Fairfield Osborn in *Our Plundered Planet*, "anyone who steals food from a groceryman's counter can be put in jail. His act hurts only the proprietor of the store. But if, for the benefit of his own pocketbook, the owner of timberlands at the head of a river strips the hills of their forests, the net result is that food is taken not from one 'proprietor' but from all the 'proprietors,' or farm owners, down the valley, because the removal of forest cover on an upper watershed will inevitably damage the water supply in the valley below, even to the point of causing the complete drying-up of wells and springs. Countless thousands of landowners in America have in this very way been brought to bankruptcy. In the face of such things, how equitable are our present moral codes?"

FOREST EDGE, MOUTH OF SURPUR CREEK

REDWOODS—GOING, GOING ON THE KLAMATH . . .

RETREATING STORM NEAR KLAMATH GLEN

BLUE CREEK, KLAMATH REDWOODS

GROVE ON THE KLAMATH

BULL CREEK AFTER THE FLOOD

. . . AND GONE AT BULL CREEK

Logging stripped the steep canyons and slopes in the upper watershed and fire completed the devastation. In the storm of December 1955, earth, boulders, and logging debris were swept from the denuded slopes into Bull Creek. A peaceful stream became a raging torrent and in a few hours toppled more than three hundred giant Redwoods in Bull Creek Flat.

UPPER BULL CREEK WATERSHED

LOGGING ALONG MILL CREEK, JUST ABOVE JEDEDIAH SMITH REDWOODS STATE PARK

Another Bull Creek tragedy in the making?

OLD HIGHWAY THROUGH THE HUMBOLDT REDWOODS

FREEWAY, HUMBOLDT REDWOODS

"New vistas" were opened—but where is the forest?

THE FREEWAY THREAT

FREEWAY CONSTRUCTION NEAR HUMBOLDT REDWOODS STATE PARK

*Trees designed for the shelter of a forest are
left vulnerable to wind. Subsurface flow is disrupted.
Alternate routes could save the forest.*

RIP-RAP, SOUTH FORK OF THE EEL RIVER

Bench-cut pattern for high-speed freeways

MODERNIZED SECTION, COAST HIGHWAY

OLD REDWOOD HIGHWAY, PRAIRIE CREEK REDWOODS STATE PARK

The road that let people see trees

The route that speeds the logging trucks

FREEWAY SWATH NEAR FOUNDERS' GROVE

FERN CANYON—IN THE WAY OF A PROPOSED FREEWAY?

In the case of Bull Creek, the devastation of the upper watershed caused no "drying-up" downstream—rather the opposite. But Osborn's principle is still valid. And in this case, the loggers took no "food" from their downstream victims. But they took something more precious, because it is rare and irreplaceable: they marred the beauty of an area that has few equals in the world. And they marred it not just for today's "proprietors . . . down the valley," they marred it for all time—for all future Californians and Americans and foreign visitors who will never see Bull Creek Flat quite as beautiful as it once was. But were the owners of the devastated lands in the upper Bull Creek watershed—or the lumber operators they employed —ever called to account? Were they ever sued for the damages they caused to the Rockefeller Forest? Were they ever even required to repair their own lands so that future harm to the state park could be minimized? Far from it. They made a nice profit on the lumber they cut—and then demanded a tidy sum before they would part with their cutover lands. "Why, this is hire and salary," as Hamlet would have cried. It is certainly an abuse, even a perversion of the privileges of private property and free enterprise. And until the law, the Forest Practice Act, is so strengthened that a landowner or logger will think twice before stripping the land—because he will be required to repair it at his own expense (as is the case in Oregon), and will be held financially liable for any damages which his misuse of the land may cause others—there will be something rotten in the State of California, and no Redwood park that does not include a complete watershed can ever be considered to be truly preserved.

This much can perhaps be said in favor of the authors of the Bull Creek tragedy: They did not foresee the end results of their logging practices. They did not set out deliberately to ruin Bull Creek Flat. Watching them at work, one might have cried, "Forgive them, for they know not what they do." But for the highly trained, efficient, methodical and forward planning operatives of the California State Division of Highways such a prayer would be of little use. For *they* know what they do—and they do it just the same.

On August 28, 1960, Governor Edmund G. Brown of California stood up before a throng of notables seated in the shadow of the Redwoods along the Avenue of the Giants, rested his fists on a lectern improvised from a Redwood stump, and spoke into the microphones as follows:

"I am privileged to speak for 15½ million Californians as we dedicate the first stage of a parkway which will lead through one of the most beautiful parts of California and the world. . . .

"We are following definite principles in our freeway program in these matchless areas. A basic premise is to open up new vistas to Californians, and our millions of visitors from other states and nations. Engineering considerations, which make this possible, are important. But it is equally sound state policy to retain scenic beauty in the unspoiled wilderness as we route freeways through the state park areas.

"What we have done here will be done elsewhere in the Redwoods—at Prairie Creek, Jedediah Smith and Richardson Grove. . . ."

God forbid!

For what was done was to *spoil* the wilderness; to "open up new vistas" that never should have been opened up; and to "route freeways through the state park areas" when by all standards of ethics such areas should have been off limits to the Highway Division's bulldozers and graders. [*There is reason to believe, however, that Governor Brown is today keenly aware of the incompatibility of high-speed freeways and the redwood parks than he was in 1960.—Ed.*]

Through parts of Humboldt Redwoods State Park there now run two parallel roadways. One is the old "Redwood Highway," now renamed the Avenue of the Giants "parkway." Along this you may still drive at a leisurely pace, your eyes straining upward through your windshield to gauge the height of the trees, whose branches often meet overhead. The traffic here is light, and it is easy to pull off the road and to step out of your car to enjoy the beauty and the quiet of the forest. But no sooner is your motor stopped than you become aware that there is no real silence here. The swish of speeding cars, the roar of lumber trucks rudely intrude upon your reverie. You look up the slope towards the source of the noise—and through a thin screen of trees you see the shapes of the cars and trucks speeding along the neighboring freeway.

The old highway almost tunnels through the forest, opening a minimum rift in the canopy overhead. It does no violence to the harmony of the landscape. From the air it is visible only when viewed from points in line with the highway's direction. The freeway is something else again. A four-lane, high-speed structure with a minimum of curves and grades, it cuts a brutal swath through the trees. "Construction of the freeway involved heavy clearing and the use of heavy logging equipment," admits a 1962 issue of *California Highways and Public Works* magazine. "The freeway traverses rugged and heavily wooded terrain." In places the slopes were gouged to many times the freeway's width with cuts and fills to prevent landslides. At one point the old highway was only a 20-foot niche in the side of a mountain. But the 60-foot freeway required a huge cut into the hill. This "Big Cut," as it is known, is hundreds of feet high and required the excavation of 1,400,000 cubic yards of dirt and rock and the felling of hundreds of giant Redwoods. Where the freeway adjoins the rivers, the natural aspect of the banks has been forever ruined. "Needless to say, considerable bank protection was involved in this 'man versus rivers' phase of the project," states another article in *California Highways.* "Combinations of heavy stone rip-rap, grouted rock, slope paving, and timber pile jetties were designed to protect new fills and turn back the rivers at points of impingement." All this and "unspoiled wilderness" too?

Indeed the freeway does "open up new vistas" — at the cost of irreparable damage to the river valley forest and serious storm "blowdown" peril to the roadside trees. And the vistas are in no way comparable to those offered by the old road. Instead of the forest closing in on all sides, majestic, mysterious, and overpowering, the trees along the freeway seem to recede into the distance, brushed aside and diminished in stature by the wide expanses of pavement and bare earth and sky, and the unique Redwoods become no more impressive than a forest of any other evergreen species.

For engineering and economic reasons, the Division of Highways found it convenient to route the freeway through portions of Humboldt Redwoods State Park— the route was more direct, and since the park lands were already owned by the State right-of-way acquisition costs were held to a minimum. Some concession was made to aesthetics by skirting some of the finer groves in the flats, and building the freeway on the slopes above them. Unfortunately even there it is damaging the forest below— damaging it not only aesthetically, by destroying its tranquillity, but physically as well. There are indications that the freeway is acting as a dam, interrupting the normal downhill seepage of groundwater and nutrients to the trees below. Many of these may be doomed as a result.

The parks farther north—Prairie Creek, Del Norte, and Jedediah Smith—have not yet been invaded by the freeway. But it looms as an ever-present threat. This threat is *imminent* in Prairie Creek, where any one of four routes considered by the Division of Highways would destroy the integrity of an intact forest-and-seashore parkland that reaches a width of nearly four miles. One route would barrel along the shore, and destroy the marvelous wild beach. Another would run just to the east, along the top of Gold Bluffs. This route would drive a permanent scar all the way through the park between beach and Redwood forest areas, and would span or fill exquisite Fern Canyon, and other natural pathways between the shore

and hinterland. Widening the present highway to freeway standards would ruin Prairie Creek itself and the best of the forest. And bringing a freeway inside the eastern edge of the park would mean the end of some of the quietest and most beautiful dedicated groves, and would require the typical, hideous fills and cuts.

There is an alternative route which would detour around the park to the east, passing entirely through logged-over land. This route would be more expensive, as it is slightly longer and would pass through private lands, thus presenting more difficulties in acquisition than would be involved in preëmpting park land. But it would offer no insuperable construction problems, it would actually benefit the park by routing fast through traffic and noisy logging and lumber trucks around it, and if the park's integrity is to be preserved this is the *only* acceptable route. Unfortunately, although the Highway people protest that no decision has been made as to the future route of this section of the freeway, a glance at the map is enough to see that the freeway stretch under construction just to the north of Prairie Creek is pointed directly at the central route through the park's heart. This does not mean a thing, Highway officials will tell you, but the Division's past performance does not allow one to repose much confidence in such assurances. Protests against threatened freeway incursions are often put off with a "Don't worry about it, we won't be doing anything here for years." Suddenly, some fine day, the bulldozers and graders show up on the scene. And any protests *then* are countered with a "You should have stated your case earlier. It's too late to change our plans now."

Compared with the Division of Beaches and Parks, the Division of Highways has almost unlimited funds. And under present statutes it possesses practically *carte blanche* to bulldoze its freeways wherever it will. It enjoys powers of eminent domain and of immediate taking, and any decision of the Highway Commission as to the public necessity of a given freeway is by law conclusive. In any showdown, Beaches and Parks are clearly outmatched. Nor are they always consulted. There is a fine stand of virgin Redwoods west of Pepperwood for which the Save-the-Redwoods League and the State parks authorities have been negotiating as an addition to the Avenue of the Giants and a memorial to Dag Hammarskjold, and which the lumber company has reserved from logging. But without even checking with the League or the Division of Beaches and Parks, the Division of Highways recently acquired a right-of-way for an extension of the freeway which would completely obliterate the western portion of this stand. Even now the trees are being felled.

Ethics, as well as aesthetics, are involved in the freeway threat to the Redwood parks. The thousands of Americans who contributed to the Save-the-Redwoods League did not intend the acres purchased with their donations to be used to speed travelling salesmen and logging trucks between Oregon and Ukiah. They gave to save Redwoods, and to save them for all time. And the State of California, in accepting title to and assuming the administration of the Redwood parks, also assumed the obligation to protect and preserve them—from fire, from logging, *and* from the freeways. Considerations of engineering and economics are secondary to this trust. There is no ethical justification for one mile of freeway in the Redwood parks: in allowing the freeway to pass through Humboldt Redwoods State Park, the State of California has been guilty of a breach of trust.

The Save-the-Redwoods League has been receiving letters of protest, even of resignation, from members who have been outraged by this breach of trust. "Why contribute money to buy land that will be despoiled by the Highway Department of the State?" asks one member. "In California where you have these Redwood forests I fail to see why you can't secure the coöperation of the Highway Department to run their roads elsewhere."

Another correspondent writes: "I am not renewing my membership in the Save-the-Redwoods League, because properties purchased through your organization go into the State Park System—with whose 'protection' I have become thoroughly disillusioned.

"What is the point of contributing to purchase of property back of Palm Springs for a 'wild area,' only to have the State authorize a commercial tramway into it—effectively destroying the character of the 'preserved' area?

"What is the point of contributing indirectly to Bliss State Park at Tahoe—only to have the State Highway Department insist on a bridge across Emerald Bay that will destroy that?

"I am sorry not to contribute again to you, but the State of California has welched on the understandings that existed when contributions have been made to 'preserve inviolate for all time these natural areas'—and until I am convinced that there will be no more fraud and deception, even if the bad faith is by other divisions of the State than the Park System, I have no intention of making any more contributions where the State of California is concerned.

"I do not think I am alone in feeling this way."

Indeed he is not. There is a growing feeling in the State that too much beauty is being sacrificed to the internal combustion engine; that too often, because it has the funds and must answer to no one on how they are spent, the Division of Highways scars the land with its freeways where there is no need for them; that the Division should obtain its funds through legislative appropriations like all other divisions of the State government; and that the Highway Commission should be required to clear its plans with men whose eye for the landscape encompasses more than the gradient of a slope or the radius of a curve. There is a feeling, in short, that the all-powerful Highway Commission must be curbed before the State strangles in the tentacles of its freeways.

Besides the thousands of "preserved" Redwoods that have fallen victim to the freeway or to erosion caused by logging, there are many more that are threatened by another kind of erosion: human erosion. In the long run, the trees' best friends could do them harm—the people who love the Redwoods enough to drive out to see them, who like to camp beneath the great trees and hike the shadowy trails.

Already, in several of the parks there is evidence that the trees are suffering from too much compaction of the soil over their shallow root systems. The growing throng of admirers who park their cars and set up their tents and walk about in the groves is slowly but surely destroying the trees. The undergrowth suffers too, to the extent that in certain areas it has practically disappeared.

This wear and tear is becoming more serious all the time, as the popularity of the Redwoods increases, as the population itself grows, and as people enjoy more and more leisure time and are increasingly inclined to spend their leisure in travel and outdoor recreation. Every year the campgrounds in the Redwood parks become more crowded. The qualities of silence and mystery and solitude that are essential components of the Redwoods' magic become increasingly impaired. The State Parks administrators have successfully resisted pressures for cheap and tawdry development of the Redwood park lands. But they must try to meet the growing public's legitimate demands for campgrounds and parking areas and toilets and trails.

The answer to this population pressure, obviously, is to expand the parks. In part, this will require the acquisition of enough additional virgin timber so that future generations may, despite their greater numbers, still find among the Redwoods something of those qualities that we can enjoy today. It will also require the acquisition of cut-over lands adjacent to today's parks, which would serve a double purpose. Protected from the continuous logging that will be standard practice on private lands, these cut-over lands will heal themselves and in a century or two should be clothed with fine stands of large trees. Provided the parks are rounded out to include whole watersheds, then these second-growth areas would protect from erosion the superlative stands in the original parks. And they could also protect them from the mounting human erosion: campgrounds and related facilities could be shifted away from the virgin stands and into the rehabilitated sections, which for those purposes would be highly acceptable substitutes.

The alternative to expanding the parks will have to be the rationing of admissions—put your name down on the list and wait until it is called two or three or five years later, as Secretary of the Interior Stewart L. Udall warned at the Wilderness Conference in San Francisco in March, 1963. Speaking of our uncontrolled proliferation and of its predictable effect on our scenic resources, he said:

". . . certain aspects of the problem are already evident. They are particularly evident here in California, where population growth is seemingly a public business of considerable pride. The San Francisco Bay Area is a prime example. Studies by the U.S. Department of Commerce indicate that the population of this region will not merely double but almost quadruple within 60 years. For every person presently living in this area, according to the statisticians, there will be three others alongside him. Will there be four times as many automobiles on the freeways? Or will there be four times as many freeways? . . .

"Of one thing we can be absolutely certain: There will not be four times as much open space available to the residents of this region. There will not be four times as many parks. . . . (And) it is a fact that if the population quadruples, we can expect that there will be far more than four times as much *demand* for open spaces, for parks, for wilderness. . . . We can consider the possibility that a quadrupled population will demand at least nine times as much outdoor recreation—nine times as much wilderness for hiking, fishing, camping, and ironically, for 'solitude.'

"Under these conditions, for every person who now hopes to camp in the summertime on the floor of Yosemite Valley, there will be an eventual nine. For every present hiker down the John Muir Trail along the spine of the Sierra, there will be nine. For every tin can and bottle and carton that now litters park and wilderness trails, there will be nine. For every hundred people on the beach at Drake's Bay, there will be at least 900 and conceivably several times that many. Here we have, in dramatic and depressing terms, the geography of rising population."

Will there be nine times as many people who will want to explore and camp in the Redwood parks? Quite possibly. But we cannot hope to save nine times as many trees as have now been set aside—there just is not that much virgin growth left. We *can* save more than we have, however. And indeed we *must*, if those trees already "saved" are to be "preserved for all time."

8. PROJECT FOR THE NATION

The well-deserved publicity that the Save-the-Red-woods League's work has enjoyed, the glowing descriptions in print and by word of mouth of the beauty of California's Redwood state parks, the photographs that are frequently published of Redwood groves illumined by the slanting rays of the sun—all tend to obscure an important fact: Of the estimated original Redwoods stand before logging began, only five per cent has been saved. "It may be that the few parks that now exist and the roadside groves sometimes left by timber companies for public relations purposes have primarily a soporific effect on the public," one writer suggested. "A normal American in a hurry is likely to experience some of the effect of a forest even without one. He may fail to notice that the Redwood forest he thinks he is driving through is not really a forest at all but may be little more than a Hollywood façade, for the trees often extend only a few hundred feet on each side of the road and are cut out in back. He may wonder briefly where all the lumber trucks are getting their trees, but he is more likely to be concerned with their clogging the highway than with their social implications. Meanwhile, in nearby forests often more vast and more magnificent than any he has seen, the chainsaws are leaving stumps and a tangle of slash and debris where majestic trees have stood for many hundreds of years."

The acreage now in state parks is insufficient to meet the future needs of our growing population. (Compare the Redwood parks' 86,723 acres with Yosemite's 760,951 acres—and Yosemite already is crowded.) It is not even enough effectively to protect the trees that *have* been "saved." More, much more needs to be done in the way of preservation before we can feel confident of the future of one of the most extraordinary and magnificent species of living things ever to have beautified the face of our planet. But if we agree that we should preserve more Redwoods, how is this to be done? The Save-the-Red-woods League and the California Division of Beaches and Parks have agreed on a master plan that would almost double the area of present Redwood state parks. But two formidable obstacles intervene: money and time.

Compared with prices on Redwood lands just a few years ago, the prices being demanded today are astronomical. Just recently, the Save-the-Redwoods League added 44 acres to Prairie Creek State Park. *The League paid as much for these 44 acres as it did for 1,500 of the park's original 6,000 acres!* And as old growth Redwoods become more scarce the stumpage price may be expected to rise still further. Given time, it is possible that the League, aided by matching State funds, could raise the money needed to complete its master plan. But time is fast running out. Some of the finest and most accessible groves, those most desirable for park purposes, are being cut now, at a rate that presages the liquidation of most privately owned virgin stands by 1980. It will serve little purpose fifteen or twenty years from now to try to raise funds for the preservation of Redwoods, for by then there will be none left to save.

If an adequate sample of the Redwood forests we have known is to be handed down by us to future generations for their inspiration and enjoyment, a very large sum of money will have to be made available for purchase of the needed acreage—and made available soon. Not ten years from now, not even five. The money must be in hand in the next year or two or three at the most, the desired lands picked out, and condemnation proceedings instituted if necessary to forestall their logging in advance of actual purchase. And as Muir would have said, "only Uncle Sam can do that."

As long ago as 1895, Professor William R. Dudley, one of the first members of the Sierra Club, urged the "immediate establishment of several Redwood parks, under the control of the United States government." His appeal went unheeded. Teddy Roosevelt, as we saw, was horrified that thousand-year-old trees should be turned into shingles, and speaking of both species of Sequoia he told a Stanford University audience: "I appeal to you . . . to protect these mighty trees, these wonderful monuments of beauty." But beyond accepting William Kent's gift of Muir Woods Roosevelt did nothing to help preserve the Redwoods. In 1919 the chief of the United States Forest Service, Colonel Henry S. Graves, visited the Humboldt and Del Norte Redwoods and impressed upon the people of those counties the irreparable loss they were sustaining by allowing the wholesale devastation of the trees. He advised State and county action to save these Redwoods, as fast as possible, but warned frankly that "as to the contribution of the Federal Government it is very likely to be delayed, and to come as aid to a project in which the State and citizens of the nation are already liberally contributing."

Prospects for a Redwoods National Park brightened in 1920—the year the Save-the-Redwoods League was incorporated—when Congress directed that a survey be made of the Redwoods region with a view to the establishment of such a park. The report on the survey, the so-called "Redington Report," was issued later in the year and recommended the purchase and establishment by the Federal Government of a 64,000 acre Redwoods National Park on the lower Klamath river drainage. Nothing came of this. Nor did anything come of the bill introduced in 1946 by Congressman Helen Gahagan Douglas of California which would have created a "Franklin Delano Roosevelt Memorial Redwood Forest" comprising most of the timberlands of the coast Redwood region. Despite certain flaws, the bill had the virtue of aiming high, a virtue often lacking in conservation efforts. As Daniel H. Burnham once said, "Make no little plans; they have no magic to stir men's blood and probably themselves will not be realized. Make big plans; aim high in hope and work, remembering that a noble, logical diagram once recorded will never die, but long after we are gone will be a living thing, asserting itself with ever-growing insistency. Remember that our sons and grandsons are going to do things that would stagger us. Let your watchword be order and your beacon beauty."

Other than the beautiful but small Muir Woods National Monument, the only Redwoods now in Federal ownership are in the Northern Redwoods Purchase Unit, adjacent to the Klamath river. Under the Weeks Act, two national forest purchase units were established including a total area of 863,000 acres. No land was ever bought in the southern unit, and only 14,000 acres in the northern. And there is at present a movement under way, backed by local timber interests (which are not local at all) to change the name of the Northern Redwoods Purchase Unit, incorporate it into the National Forest, and abolish the authority for acquiring any additional land—an authority still in force although it has not been acted on since the original purchases. As far as "preserving" the Redwoods, the NRPU has accomplished nothing. It is divided into two sections—the Experimental Forest, on which the National Forest Service is conducting cutting experiments in cooperation with a major lumber company; and the Timber Management Unit, in which the Forest Service has conducted several timber sales. With so little Redwood land in Forest Service ownership, one may well ask why *any* of it is being logged; one may question why a portion of it is being devoted to experiments which can

only benefit the large private timber holdings which surround the Purchase Unit. And when in virtually every other National Forest District there is so much stress of "multiple use," one may wonder why there is none here—no recreation development on the NRPU despite the fact that part of it adjoins the Klamath river, one of the nation's prime recreation areas.

From the days when it practically gave away the world's richest timberlands, the Federal government neglected the Redwoods. As a further instance of this neglect, for years it was realized that the entire Redwood region should be studied to reappraise its potential for a national park and for scientific research; that its ecological problems should be analyzed along with its patterns of land ownership and logging practices. But the National Park Service never was given the funds for such a survey. At last in May 1963 the funds were made available—though not by the Federal Government but by the National Geographic Society, which for almost 50 years has played an active role in the saving of both species of Sequoia. "The real urgency to save one of our greatest natural assets seems to involve Federal participation: (1) in the purchase of lands, and (2) the possibility of establishing a Redwoods National Park," Secretary of the Interior Udall declared. "Through the National Geographic Society's generous grant of $64,000 . . . we are now able to move ahead on a study urgently needed to determine the most effective means of preserving an adequate segment of Redwood forest—to guarantee their protection and provide for their appropriate use and enjoyment by the public."

The condition for Federal aid once described by Colonel Graves, that the saving of the Redwoods be a "project in which the State and citizens of the nation are already liberally contributing," long has been met. And what could be more fitting than that the Federal government should at long last play a significant role in the preservation of this national treasure? For the Redwoods are no more of purely local interest to Californians than the Grand Canyon is to Arizonans. They are an asset to the whole nation. Indeed they are one of the wonders of the world, and as such they belong to the world.

The most glowing report that might issue from the current survey will not of course ensure that the Federal Government will act—the "Redington Report" was glowing enough yet led nowhere, except to the extent that it influenced the Save-the-Redwoods League's plans. Opposition to the necessary large Federal expenditures can be expected from certain "economy"-minded politicians, who will care little that all the generations of the future would be grateful to the 88th or 89th Congress for having authorized this expenditure. Like Stalin, who once asked about the Pope, "How many divisions does he have?", such lawmakers think of future generations in terms of "How many votes do they have?" Opposition may come from certain county officials who will cry about "withdrawing private lands from the tax roll." And opposition is most likely from the Redwood lumber industry which may protest that it is being driven to the wall.

But for both county officials and lumbermen the purchase by the Federal Government of a large acreage of Redwood timberlands would only somewhat hasten a doomsday that in any case is less than 20 years away. After 1980, what? After all virgin timber has been liquidated, how will the counties obtain their revenues? By tax policies which encourage—nay, force—the cutting of standing timber are they not advancing the day they must come to grips with this question? Would it not be more sensible for the counties in the Redwood region to hang on to as much of the virgin Redwood growth as possible, and count on the growing tourist trade attracted by the trees—especially if a national park can be established—to bring in a dependable and constantly increasing flow of revenue? In speeding the liquidation of the Redwoods, by far their biggest attraction, are not the local counties literally undermining their future and eliminating the one big new source of income they can fall back on once the big timber is gone? (Of course the Federal Government,

if it decides to set up a park, can ease the transition for the counties by paying them an annual sum equivalent to the lost taxes until such time as increased tourist revenues make up the loss.)

As for the industry, in 20 years or less it will have to fall back on second growth timber. If the government buys a sizeable acreage of the remaining virgin growth, the industry might have to make the conversion in 15 years or 10. But it would be fully compensated for the lumber it would lose—and would be spared the costs of cutting and processing it. How then could the industry argue it was being put out of business—unless it were secretely convinced that there is no profit in second-growth Redwood, present protestations about "selective cutting" and "perpetual yield" notwithstanding?

The industry would have to make adjustments, but it is hard to see how the establishment of a large Federal preserve in the Redwoods would do it much harm. The counties, too, would have to adjust, but in the end they would profit greatly. The coming generations would have everything to gain. And above all, the preservation of one of Nature's noblest achievements is an obligation which must be fulfilled now or never—and Federal action may be our last chance to fulfill it. As Secretary Udall put it, "When the results of the year-long study are announced—probably next spring—we must be ready to act. Along with our power to destroy, let us hope that we have the infinite wisdom to protect. The Redwoods have waited a long time, but now time is running out."

9. EPILOGUE—OR EPITAPH?

Tall and straight the last Redwoods stand, while we debate their fate. They are our captives; their death has been decreed. There still is time to stay the execution—but time is running short. If we debate too long we will, discover that the executioner has taken the decision from our hands: His axe will have claimed those lives we could have spared.

It is somehow preposterous that we of this generation—we of this decade, even—should have the power to reprieve or condemn a race which Nature has preserved over more than 100,000,000 years. There is something frighteningly presumptuous about a man, his lifespan limited to a few decades, who strides up to a Redwood which has seen a thousand summers and might see as many more, and in an hour's hacking and sawing brings the giant down.

Indeed there are many who feel that any further logging of virgin Redwood is simply immoral, and would stop using Redwood and look for substitutes rather than complete the destruction of these incomparable trees. One such citizen was Madison Grant, who wrote: "It is scarcely necessary to dwell on the crime involved in the destruction of the oldest trees on earth. The cutting of a Sequoia for grape stakes or railroad ties is like breaking up one's grandfather's clock for kindling to save the trouble of splitting logs at the woodpile, or lighting one's pipe with a Greek manuscript to save the trouble of reaching for the matches.

"After the fall of the Roman Empire the priceless works of classic art were 'needed' for lime, and statues were slacked down for this purpose, but the men who did it are today rightly dubbed 'vandals and barbarians.' What then will the next generation call us if we continue to destroy these priceless trees because lumber is 'needed' for grape stakes and railroad ties?"

If by some freak we were to come across, in some hitherto unexplored corner of the world, a surviving herd of dinosaurs, a species contemporary with the earliest Redwoods, would we seek to preserve it or would we kill it off for its hides or its meat or its carcasses? Quite possibly the latter, for it has always been man's bent to reduce Nature's myriad marvels to their lowest common denominator—human "needs." And he has always justified this attitude with the self-serving assumption that God made the earth for man to enjoy. What man finds useful is by definition "good." What he has no use for is worthless and probably evil. "What good is it?" (meaning "What good is it to me?") shrugs man as he brings his heel down on a toad in his garden—although the toad may consume the insects that attack his flowers.

Because we are clever, we find ever new ways to "push Nature around" so as to fit her to our "needs." Because we are not clever enough, or foresighted enough, to halt the multiplication of our numbers we find we have ever greater "needs" to meet and must push Nature that much harder. And so we make constantly increasing demands on the resources of our nonexpanding planet. We remake our landscape to conform to man-made patterns. And what it gains in "usefulness" it loses in diversity and beauty.

Arizona "needs" more water for its booming population—and the fantastically beautiful gorge of Glen Canyon is dammed and drowned in silty water while other proposed dams threaten to mutilate Grand Canyon itself. (But does Arizona really "need" these extra million citizens?) The San Francisco Bay Area "needs" more land for homes and industry—and one of the world's great bays shrinks yearly as its shallows are filled. Northern California "needs" a new freeway to accommodate growing motor traffic between San Francisco and Crescent City, and thousands of irreplaceable Redwoods are sacrificed to the automobile.

Often the so-called "needs" are spurious—mere creations of promotion and advertising. Paris couturiers decree that the well-dressed woman "needs" a coat of Somali leopard. And while the magnificent beasts are exterminated the women's pages unblushingly feature the pelts, the furriers stock them, and women buy them. It matters little that a woman can be both warm and chic in a coat made of some material that does not threaten a species with extinction. Advertising and promotion—and the undoubted handsomeness of the product—have boomed Redwood as a material for sidings and panelling and "decks" and patios, and Redwood houses as a result enjoy a tremendous vogue. Of course homes just as splendid and just as modern are being built of other materials that do not require the chopping down of the world's most beautiful and fastest-dwindling virgin forests.

But "man does not live by bread alone." He has needs

In a too-crowded, too-synthetic new world, man still has some simple, ancient needs:

a hunger for solitude, a thirst for beauty, a craving for wildness.

MAIL RIDGE, HUMBOLDT COUNTY

It is fair to remember that
  this is not a land that belongs to us.
  We cannot destroy it without destroying something in us.
Its trees can teach us tenacity
  and patience and serenity and respect.
Life's urge to survive is the force
  that shaped them and their world of wildness,
  that made them one of the great miracles. . . .

ROOSEVELT ELK, PRAIRIE CREEK REDWOODS STATE PARK

Man, if he is too impatient to care,
    can end this miracle, can terminate a chain of life
    going back without interruption to an old eternity
    when life first strove to leave the mother sea.

Or man, able to create ideas, can meet his old material needs with a different urge—

an urge to preserve what he cannot replace.

Wildness made man but he cannot make it. He can only spare it.

that are no less real and no less vital—although they are harder to measure in economic terms—than food and water and shelter. He has a thirst for beauty. He often has a hunger for solitude. He craves the companionship of other animal species. He has a deep, atavistic urge for identification with Nature. Witness the extraordinary upsurge of hiking and camping and boating and the overwhelming increase in use of our national parks.

Unfortunately, we too often take things for granted until they get scarce. We begin to worry about a bird or an animal only when suddenly we realize it is becoming extinct. Only now, when our unspoiled wilderness is down to isolated fragments, are we beginning to realize how much we miss its former glory, and are we trying to preserve what little is left. Such regrets are frequently too late. We may mourn the demise of the passenger pigeon but nothing will bring it back to life. We might be tempted to dynamite Glen Canyon Dam but it would be too late: the muddy waters impounded behind it would already have ruined forever the canyon they had drowned. We might wish we could raze Los Angeles' sprawling suburbs; but whatever else this might accomplish it would not bring back the orange groves.

With the last Redwoods, we still have a chance. But to preserve what we already have "saved" we have to save more. And in fairness to our grandchildren and *their* grandchildren we have to save *still* more. The survey of the Redwood region being made by the National Park Service, the interest shown by the Administration in the possible establishment of a Redwoods National Park, offer us our best and perhaps last chance to preserve "for all time" an adequate and representative segment of the "world's finest forest."

If through indolence, indifference or misguided "economy" we let pass this chance, our generation, which already has allowed the sacrifice of so much natural beauty to the false gods of "growth" and "progress," will go down in history as the one which allowed the last of the virgin Redwoods to be sold down the Eel and the Klamath and the Smith rivers and converted into commercial products for which substitutes were on hand.

We are grateful for the preservation that was achieved, even though it did not quite come up to the dream. We ourselves may yet earn the gratitude of those to come, *if* we become aroused at the desecration of the world's finest forest, *if* we bring the weight of our collective indignation —our own and that of the government that serves us—to bear, *if* we insist that the ever-living Sequoias shall indeed live on.

BIBLIOGRAPHY

BOOKS

Anonymous. *California, Where Life Is Better.* Californians, Inc., San Francisco, 1923.

Baker, Richard St. Barbe. *Among the Trees.* John Swain & Sons, Ltd., London, 1935.

———. *The Redwoods.* L. Drummond, Ltd., London, 1945.

Berry, Edward Wilbur. *Tree Ancestors: A Glimpse into the Past.* Williams and Wilkins Company, Baltimore, 1923.

Bolton, Herbert E. *Anza's California Expeditions.* University of California Press, Berkeley, 1930.

Bowers, Nathan A. *Cone-bearing Trees of the Pacific Coast.* Pacific Books, Palo Alto, 1942.

Brewer, William H. *Up and Down California in 1860-1864.* University of California Press, Berkeley, 1949.

Bryant, Harold C. *Outdoor Heritage.* Powell Publishing Company, Los Angeles, 1929.

Chaney, Ralph W. *Redwoods of the Past.* Save-the-Redwoods League, San Francisco, 1934.

Chase, Joseph S. *California Coast Trails.* Houghton Mifflin Company, Boston, 1913.

Clar, C. Raymond. *California Government and Forestry.* Division of Forestry, Sacramento, 1959.

Collingwood, G. H., and Warren D. Brush. *Knowing Your Trees.* American Forestry Association, Washington, D.C., 1937, 1958, 1963.

Crow, John A. *California As a Place to Live.* Charles Scribner's Sons, New York, 1953.

Drury, Aubrey. *California: An Intimate Guide.* Harpers, New York, 1947.

Drury, Wells and Aubrey. *California Tourist Guide and Handbook: Authentic Description of Routes of Travel and Points of Interest In California.* Western Guidebook Company, Berkeley, 1913.

Encyclopedia Americana.

Encyclopedia Britannica.

Fritz, Emanuel (compiler). *California Coast Redwood: An Annotated Bibliography.* Foundation for American Resource Management, San Francisco, 1957.

———. *The Story Told by a Fallen Redwood.* Save-the-Redwoods League, San Francisco, 1934.

Gannett, Lewis. *Sweet Land.* Doubleday, New York, 1934.

Jepson, Willis L. *Silva of California.* The University Press, Berkeley, 1910.

———. *The Trees of California.* Sather Gate Bookshop, Berkeley, 1923.

———. *Trees, Shrubs and Flowers of the Redwood Region.* Save-the-Redwoods League, San Francisco, 1935.

Johnson, Arthur T. *California: An Englishman's Impressions of the Golden State.* Duffield & Company, New York, 1913.

Kroeber, Alfred L. *Handbook of the Indians of California.* Smithsonian Institution, Bureau of Ethnology, Bulletin 78, Government Printing Office, Washington, D.C., 1925.

McNairn, Jack, and Jerry MacMullen. *Ships of the Redwood Coast.* Stanford University Press, Palo Alto, California, 1945.

Merriam, John C. *The Garment of God; Influence of Nature in Human Experience.* Charles Scribner's Sons, New York, 1943.

———. *The Highest Use of the Redwoods.* Save-the-Redwoods League, San Francisco, 1941.

———. *The Living Past.* Charles Scribner's Sons, New York, 1930.

———. *The Tasks Ahead of the Save-the-Redwoods League.* Save-the-Redwoods League, San Francisco, 1934.

Muir, John. *Our National Parks.* Houghton Mifflin Company, Boston, 1901.

Pardee, George C. *History of California.* Century History Company, New York, 1914.

Peattie, Donald Culross. In *A Natural History of Western Trees.* Houghton Mifflin Company, Boston, 1950, 1953.

———. *The Pacific Coast Ranges.* Vanguard Press, New York, 1946.

Powers, Alfred. *Redwood Country.* Duell, Sloan & Pearce, New York, 1949.

Robinson, John, and Alfred Calais. *State Parks of California.* Lane Book Company, Menlo Park, 1961.

Roosevelt, Theodore. *Addresses and Messages,* pp. 188-198. G. P. Putnam's Sons, New York, 1904.

Save-the-Redwoods League. *Bibliography of the Redwoods.* Save-the-Redwoods League, San Francisco, 1935.

Shankland, Robert. *Steve Mather of the National Parks.* Alfred A. Knopf, New York, 1951.

Shirley, James Clifford. *The Redwoods of Coast and Sierra.* University of California Press, Berkeley, 1937.

Strybing Arboretum Society. *The Redwood Trail.* Strybing Arboretum Society of Golden Gate Park, San Francisco, 1963.

Taylor, Norman. *The Ageless Relicts.* St. Martins Press, New York, 1962.

Tilden, Freeman. *The State Parks: Their Meaning in American Life.* Alfred A. Knopf, New York, 1962.

Weaver, Harriett E. *There Stand the Giants: The Story of the Redwood Trees.* Lane Book Company, Menlo Park, 1960.

ARTICLES

Anonymous, "In a Redwood Logging Camp," *Harper's New Monthly Magazine,* January, 1883.

Benedict, H. W. "Redwood Freeway," *California Highways and Public Works,* January-February, 1962.

Bonner, W. G. "The Trail in the Redwoods," *Overland Monthly,* June, 1901.

Closson, Mabel H. "Humboldt Lumbering," *Overland Monthly,* August, 1893.

Douglas, Helen Gahagan. "The Proposed Roosevelt Redwood Forest," *National Parks Magazine,* April-June, 1947.

Drury, Aubrey. "The Avenue of the Giants and Beyond," *The Living Wilderness*, May, 1943.

Drury, Newton B. "Preserving the Native Landscape in California," *National Parks Bulletin*, July, 1940.

————. "Transmuting Science into Conservation," *Cooperation in Research*, Carnegie Institution of Washington Publication No. 501, pages 753-763, 1938.

Eames, Ninetta. "Staging in the Mendocino Redwoods," *Overland Monthly*, August and September, 1892.

Fritz, Emanuel. "The Changes I Have Seen," *Humboldt Times*, March 7, 1963.

————. "The Life and Habits of Redwood the Extraordinary," California Redwood Association, November, 1960.

Grant, J. D. "Redwoods—Ever-Living Memorials," *American Forests and Forest Life*, 1929.

Graves, Henry Solon. "Our Most Urgent Public Park," *American Forests and Forest Life*, February, 1926.

Knight, Emerson. "The Del Norte Coast State Park," Sierra Club *Bulletin*, 1931.

Lane, D. R. "Empire of Giants, the Redwood Parks," *Motorland*, November-December, 1957.

Linden, Grace. "The Prairie Creek Redwoods," *Natural History*, March-April, 1932.

McCrackin, Josephine Clifford. "About the Big Basin," *Overland Monthly*, August, 1900.

Muir, John. "Save the Redwoods," Sierra Club *Bulletin*, Vol. 11, no. 1, 1920.

Osborn, Henry Fairfield. "Sequoia—the Auld Lang Syne of Trees," *Natural History*, Vol. 19, no. 6, 1919.

Save-the-Redwoods League. *Annual Reports*, 1920 through 1950.

————. *News Bulletins* (issued several times a year), 1941 through 1963.

Sunset. "Autumn in the Northern Redwoods," *Sunset Magazine*, October, 1960.

————. "Forest Walking and Forest Camping," *Sunset Magazine*, September, 1963.

Walter, Carrie Stevens. "The Preservation of the Big Basin," *Overland Monthly*, October, 1902.

PHOTOGRAPHERS

The numbers following each photographer's name refer to the pages on which his work is represented:

ANSEL ADAMS: 36, 51, 78 & 79.

California Division of Beaches and Parks: 98.

MADISON DEVLIN: 58 (top).

Fremont Art Company: 52 & 53.

FLORENCE HARRISON: 55 (bottom).

PHILIP HYDE: 2, 4 & 5, 6, 7, 8 & 9, 16, 21, 22, 23, 24, 26, 27, 28, 33, 34 & 35, 37, 38, 42, 44, 56 (bottom left and right), 57 (bottom), 59 (top), 61, 63, 64 & 65, 66 (bottom), 76, 77 (top and bottom), 81, 82, 83, 84 & 85, 86, 95, 99, 100, 101, 105 (bottom), 106, 107, 117, 118, 119, 120 & 121, 122 & 123, 124.

Moulin Studios: 55 (top), 80, 108.

Redwood and Lumbering in California Forests, San Francisco, Edgar Cherry & Co., Publishers, 1884. 54 (top, center and bottom), 55 (center).

HARVEY RICHARDS: 59 (bottom), 66 (top).